Mastering Golf

Lou Graham
with John Bibb

 Contemporary Books, Inc.
Chicago

Library of Congress Cataloging in Publication Data

Graham, Lou.
    Mastering golf.

    Includes index.
    1. Golf.   I. Bibb, John, joint author.   II. Title.
GV965.G683   796.352'3   77-91155
ISBN 0-8092-7763-8
ISBN 0-8092-7761-1 pbk.

Published by Contemporary Books, Inc.
180 North Michigan Avenue, Chicago, Illinois 60601
Manufactured in the United States of America
Library of Congress Catalog Card Number: 77-91155
International Standard Book Number: 0-8092-7763-8 (cloth)
                                    0-8092-7761-1 (paper)

Published simultaneously in Canada by
Beaverbooks
953 Dillingham Road
Pickering, Ontario L1W 1Z7
Canada

Dedication

To my dad, Martin, who taught me to play the game, and to Patsy, who encouraged me to play it well.

Contents

1

The Game

"Mister Graham, tell us how you could make such a hard shot and then miss such an easy putt."

The question came from an upturned freckled face, squinting beneath a size-too-large golf visor. The little guy was sitting cross-legged in the front row, listening to every word during the Tennessee PGA Junior Golf Academy lecture series. The clinic was held a week or so after the 1977 U.S. Open in Tulsa.

He was asking about my fourth-round performance on the 17th hole at Southern Hills Country Club. That's when I came out of the woods—thanks to the best competitive shot of my life—and then blew an eight-foot birdie putt.

The miss conceivably cost me a second U.S. Open championship in three years. That's what my friends like to tell me, but deep down I know such speculation is most presumptive. Hubert Green was playing such super golf that afternoon—under such abnormal circumstances—that I figure he would have done whatever he had to do to win, regardless of what was happening to me and my putter on the 17th.

At any rate, it was as candid a question as has ever been put to me about golf. Even the crustiest golf writer I know never put it to me that way. I stammered and hemmed and hawed for an answer. Finally, I played it safe: "Well, golf's funny that way." It didn't seem like much of an answer, but it satisfied the little rascal.

Now, in retrospect, I believe in that single sentence I summed up the game of golf. That's real presumption, isn't it? It sounds so much better, I suppose, if you say it like Gary Player does: "Golf is a humbling game."

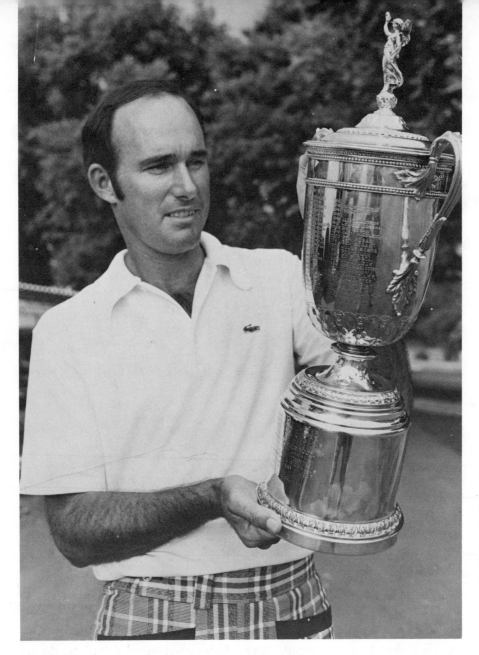

Lou Graham's U.S. Open record, headlined by his championship at Chicago's Medinah in 1975, also includes a tie for third in 1974 at Winged Foot, New York, and second to Hubert Green by one shot in the 1977 tournament in Tulsa. (Photo by Gerald Holly)

Either description, Gary's or mine, means the same thing. It means golf can be the most exasperating, unpredictable, unenjoyable game in the world. Or, it can produce some of the most exciting, challenging, memorable hours in a person's life. It's like going to college. A student gets out of it exactly what he or she puts into it.

In these pages I hope to offer suggestions that will help ease some of the frustrations that spoil the game for many. Or perhaps this book will present a tip or two that will save a stroke now and then, adding zest for those who love and enjoy golf for what it really is to me: just a game.

I believe everybody who plays golf began to play because it looked like fun. It even looked easy. I think it is important to keep the fun aspect in mind. The problem with so many players is that they lose sight of what's really happening when they swing a golf club at a golf ball.

Almost everybody, at one time or another, has taken a stick or broom handle and swung at a pebble or walnut or tin can. Furthermore, almost everybody enjoyed reasonable success at moving the pebble, walnut, or can along an intended path. But let that broom handle suddenly become a 3-iron and that walnut a golf ball, and the weirdest things imaginable begin to happen.

Under such circumstances I have seen

grown men cry. I have seen young men oath the parentage of lifelong companions. I have seen women let dinner burn and eventually give up their families. I have seen men skip dinner, lose their jobs, and ultimately their self-respect. All this, in pursuit of a par round!

The relatively simple act of swinging a stick at an object somehow becomes so confused that the harder you swing, the more incredible becomes the result of the action. You hit down on the golf ball, and it goes up. You hit the ball on an upward angle, and it goes down. You swing at it from right to left, and the ball goes left-to-right. You try it the other way, hitting toward the right, and it goes left.

As I told the little boy in Tennessee: "Golf's funny that way."

But don't despair. I believe everybody possesses certain natural movements that are vital parts of the golf swing. My idea is to avoid interfering with those natural movements and concentrate on implementing what we already have in our favor. I'll offer what I believe are some simple, hopefully easy-to-understand, tips that have helped me learn to play and shave a shot or two off a round now and then. Later on, I'll show you how these tips and my understanding of the game actually came into play on that last round in Tulsa.

At the start, I believe a player should be exposed to the basics of the swing—the grip, the address, stance, takeaway, downswing, and follow-through—all at once. That's because I believe everybody knows how to hit a rock with a stick. It's a one-piece deal, a rhythmical motion. It's like sitting in a rocking chair. Everything should be s-l-o-w and s-m-o-o-t-h. Nothing should be rushed. No conscious effort should be made to speed or slow the swing.

Think about it. You hit that rock while walking. Imagine hitting a golf ball on the run! Chances are you could hit the rock while holding the stick in one hand—either hand, at that—and it certainly was no big deal.

Well, that's what this book might do for you. All I'm going to try to do is put your hands on the "stick" in a position which should furnish you with better control and more power to propel the "rock" farther. I want to put your feet in an alignment that will help you hit the "rock" on a more accurate line.

When you arrive at the proper tempo of bringing the club away from the ball and back into and through it, you are on your own. Tempo is important, because it is your very own. Julius Boros's swing is much slower than Doug Sanders's, and mine is a different speed from either. It's a matter of confidence.

I suggest practice, but don't hesitate to play when it is convenient. Don't lose the fun of golf by spending all your time on the practice tee. If you are new to the game, play it. The enthusiasm you have at the outset adds to your drive to learn to play.

Rookie players might look around for a senior golfing pal, and there are more of these delightful people now than ever before. I recommend seniors for the young players because many seniors love to talk the game, and they have the time, and generally the patience, to help a new golfer learn.

If you've been at the game a while and think you've "found something" that will help chop off a stroke or two, get to the practice tee and try it. I believe you also can make adjustments right on the course when you're playing for the drinks. I even change my game during a competitive round occasionally.

I made adjustments at Tulsa on the last day, and they came within a stroke of getting me in a play-off with Hubert. We'll talk about those changes.

2
The Hands

I believe the hands are probably the most important part of a successful golf game, and every effort should be made to get the hands set on the club correctly for each shot.

THE GRIP

The grip is difficult to learn. There are very few players with what I would call the perfect grip, but the real superstars are the golfers who have grips that remain the same, year in and year out. I think it is the grip that is the chief difference between the top players and the others.

To each his own, but for me the proper grip is taken by placing the left hand on the club so that the club crosses the left forefinger at the middle of the finger and angles up the hand. The heel of the left hand rests on the shaft. The fingers are then closed on the shaft. The left thumb is placed down—not straight down—and slightly to the right side of the shaft, or away from the direction of flight.

I suggest the use of the overlapping grip. That's where the little finger on the right hand goes over the forefinger of the left hand. The shaft runs across the middle of the forefinger of the right hand. The grip of the right hand is in the fingers. The pad at the heel of the right thumb is placed on top of the left thumb.

When you look down at the grip you should see two knuckles of the left hand and the famous V which is formed between the thumb and forefinger of the right hand. This V should point toward the area between your neck and your right shoulder.

The firm, or pressure, points of the grip begin with the little finger on the left hand. The three little fingers on the shaft control

The left hand goes on the club first, with the index, or forefinger, going under the shaft and then pointing up the hand.

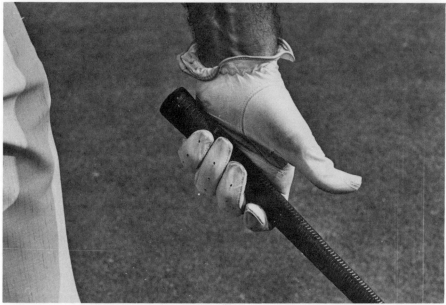

The heel of the left hand rests on the shaft, and the three remaining fingers grip the club and are the pressure points for the left hand during the swing.

The left thumb is placed down the shaft, slightly to the right side of the grip, or away from the direction of flight. (Photos by Jimmy Holt)

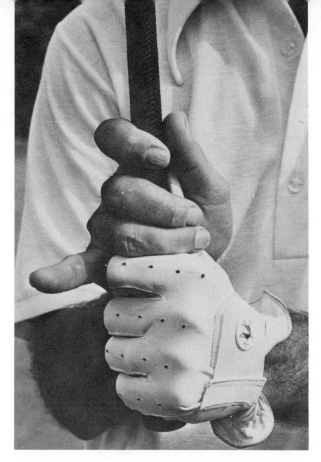

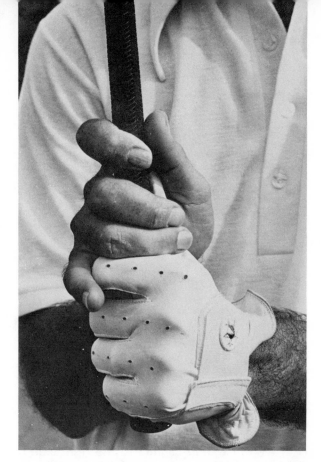

Graham prefers the overlapping grip, where the little finger of the right hand is placed over and across the forefinger of the left.

The grip of the right hand is in the fingers, with the pad at the heel of the right thumb placed on top of the left thumb.

The forefinger and thumb of the right hand provide a pressure point because of their pinching action which actually places the club face on the ball. (Photos by Jimmy Holt)

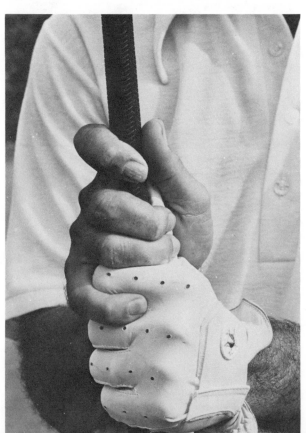

the club at the top of the swing. It is important therefore that you have a firm grip in the three little fingers of the left hand. If these fingers break away from the shaft, the club head drops at the top of the swing, and the grip must be reset as you bring the club down toward the ball.

It is no trouble to reset the grip, mind you. Indeed, it can be reset anywhere from the top of the swing to the moment of impact. That is the problem. The grip cannot be reset at precisely the same spot on each swing. The result is an ever-so-slight turning or twisting of the club head. This wobbling produces those goofy-looking shots we were talking about earlier. So remember to hang onto the club tightly with those three little fingers on the left hand.

A lot of people say the main pressure point in the right hand lies in the two large fingers (middle and ring). Maybe, but I have always

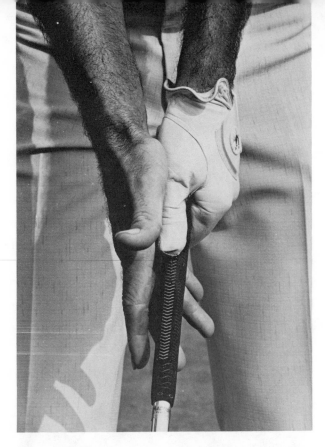

With his left thumb slightly to the right side of the shaft, Graham begins to put his grip together and form the famous inverted V with his right hand.

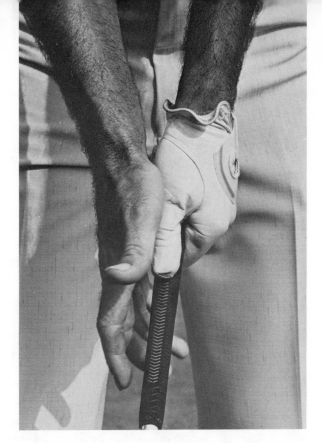

The pad at the heel of the right thumb is placed on top of the left thumb.

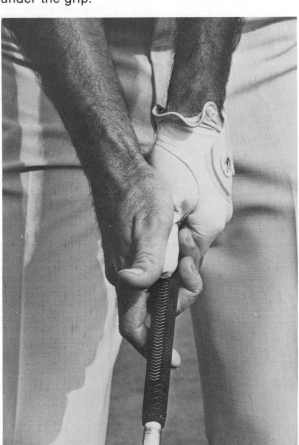

The shaft runs across the forefinger of the right hand as the other three fingers begin to curl under the grip.

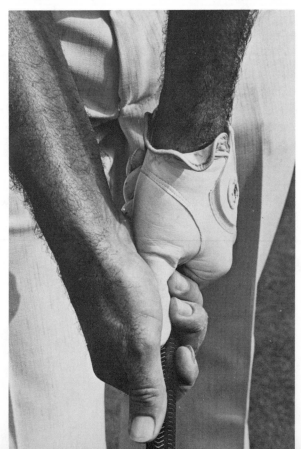

The first two knuckles on the left hand show clearly when Graham's right hand moves on top of the club.

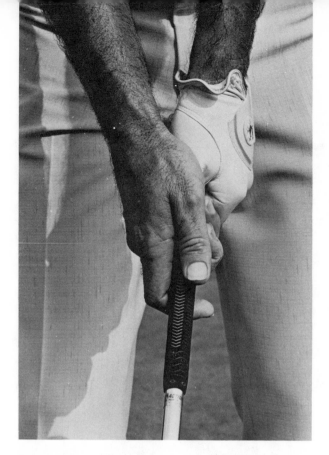

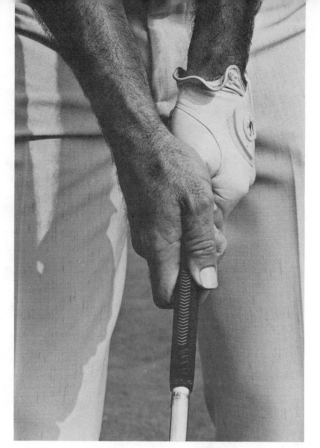

The inverted V becomes visible as the fingers and thumbs of both hands draw the grip snug.

Graham considers the primary pressure point of the right hand relies on the thumb and forefinger forming the V which points upward to an area between the neck and right shoulder. (Photos by Jimmy Holt)

felt I have more control of the club by relying on the thumb and forefinger of the right hand.

Of course, the proper grip is a combination of all the fingers. I have a good, firm grip with the left hand in the three fingers, but I also have the thumb and forefinger of the right hand tightly on the shaft. The thumb-forefinger pinching action actually places the club face on the ball. That's where I feel that you really get the touch, as in hitting a chip. I use this same grip for all shots except putting.

Players like to change their grips for chipping, but I feel the one I have described is strong enough for the big strokes, yet sensitive enough for those delicate little shot-saving ones around the greens.

EXERCISE

Naturally, a good grip requires strong hands, and strong hands require exercise. It makes sense to follow a regular exercise routine aimed toward strengthening the hands, wrists, and forearms.

I think the exercise which helps me most is one that may be carried out even while playing. I also use it regularly at home during the winter or in the motel room when I have a golf club available.

I take a club and hold it in my hand by the grip. Just hold it out there straight. Then, I begin to twist it. I turn it clockwise for a while and then counterclockwise. First I use the right hand, then the left. I spin the club, holding it straight out and turning it around and around by regripping for each fraction of the twist. You get the same effect as though you are using a hand exerciser to strengthen your forearm and hand. By using a golf club, you are actually feeling the club balance and

An exercise Graham uses to strengthen arms, wrists, and hands is twisting—by regripping—a golf club extended from his waist. The club is turned clockwise and counterclockwise in both the right and left hands. (Photo by Jimmy Holt)

learning to feel the dead weight of the club more.

This twisting exercise may be done as you walk along the fairway between shots, but I caution you not to overdo it on the course because it can be very tiring. Try using it while you are waiting on the first tee. I have found it to be a most reliable exercise.

INJURIES

The only injury I ever had in golf was to my left hand. In 1969 I had to leave the tour because of tendinitis. The surgery was successful, which makes me grateful that my doctor liked medical school as much as I liked college golf. One of the exercises prescribed after surgery was to squeeze a chunk of foam rubber, a tennis ball, or a hand exerciser. I am happy to say I have never had any serious problems with my hand since the surgery.

There was one time at Augusta when I experienced some pain in my hand. The incident reminds me of another tip I will pass along right now: Don't try to carry three traveling clothes bags with one hand.

3
The Feet

In my opinion, more off-line shots are hit because of improper alignment than any other error.

I have always felt the proper address begins by moving the right foot to the line of play. After the right foot is set, bring in the left one and adjust your stance over the ball.

THE DRIVER

I like to play the ball about two inches inside the left heel on all shots except the driver. The driver is played forward—maybe up around the arch of the foot—but really where it feels best for you. It should be no farther back in your stance than the two-inch margin inside the left heel.

THE STANCE FOR IRONS

On short iron shots, you hear people say the ball is located farther back toward the right foot. I do not believe this is correct. The ball is kept inside the left foot, still by a couple of inches. You get the impression that the ball has moved to the right, but what really happens is that you take a more narrow stance.

In other words, the ball's position in relation to the left foot does not change. Instead, the right foot is brought up closer toward the left. The ball however keeps its same position.

With longer shots, the stance is wider, and again it is not the ball but the right foot that moves. The ball stays right there—two inches inside the left heel—and the right foot moves away, widening the distance between the feet and opening the way for a longer swing.

Tips about Irons

An important point to keep in mind when

Positioning of the ball with respect to the left foot shows that Graham keeps the ball approximately two inches inside the left heel. When hitting a driver, Graham says the ball may move forward toward the left arch, but never back past the two-inch margin from the heel. (Photo by Jimmy Holt)

With both feet square to the line of flight, Graham demonstrates the proper alignment at address. The left foot points ever so slightly toward the target on irons, and turns a little more toward the target on wood shots. For a hook stance, Graham's right foot comes away from the intended straightaway line. For a fade stance, Graham's left foot moves back off the line. (Photo by Jimmy Holt)

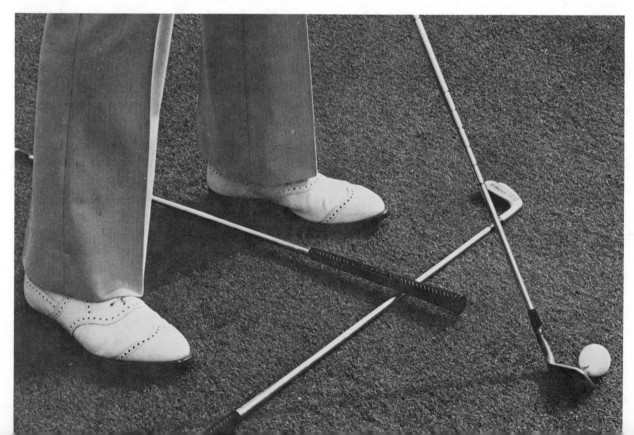

playing good iron shots is to swing the club and not try to hit the ball hard. A lot of people try to hit their long irons harder because they figure they have to get more distance. However, you should let the iron do your work.

You are taking a longer backswing with longer irons, and therefore you are creating more clubhead speed. The longer the iron, the bigger the arc in your swing. The clubhead has to travel farther to get to the ball and there is more speed at impact, thus more power. The lower loft on the long irons sends the ball off the club face on a lower trajectory. The ball goes farther, rather than higher. Therefore, on the long iron shots take a wider stance, take a longer swing, and let the clubhead do the rest.

Another mistake made frequently on long iron shots is attempting to pick the ball up off the grass rather than hitting down and through the shot.

With a long iron, hit with a sweeping motion, a movement similar to the one used for wood shots. Hit down on the ball, take a light divot, and drive the clubhead through the shot. Extend the sweeping motion right on through the ball. The main thing is to not try to force any distance out of a club. Just swing the club.

HOOKS AND FADES

Sooner or later, every player faces the test of attempting to hit a golf shot when the ball must travel from right to left (the draw or hook shot) or left to right (the fade or cut shot).

If you are going to play a hook, the right foot moves off the straight line of flight. The right foot is now behind the left foot and this creates the familiar closed stance. In theory it is now easier to swing from inside out across the line of flight. From this approach the spin imparted from clubhead to golf ball makes the ball move right to left.

I differ from some professionals in the way I play the real big hook shot, the shot you try to hit when you want a rolling, distance-gathering hook. On this shot—maybe to get around a tree or a dogleg where there is plenty of room—I like to open my stance by moving the left foot back away from the line of flight. This position helps me get into the shot and get the left side of my body out of the way quickly. The clubhead rolls over in a pronating fashion, creating a great deal of hook spin on the ball.

My natural shot has always been the draw. There are times however when I need to execute the cut shot, forcing spin on the ball that makes it travel from left to right.

On the cut shot, the first move is to aim left of the target. Next, take the club slightly on the outside of the straight line of flight and cut across the ball as you come into it. One of the important parts of hitting a good cut shot is to keep your weight at impact on the left side. As you move into the shot, be sure to get your weight on the left foot so that the club is cutting across (outside-in) the line of play, thus putting the desired spin on the shot.

If you don't get the weight to the left for a cut shot, or if you put the weight too far on the right side as you move in, the tendency is to turn over on the ball and pull it to the left. If this happens, you have big troubles, because instead of getting a cut shot that goes to the right, you may come up with a double-cross, a hook that goes to the left—way to the left, I might add.

I have hit my share of these double-cross shots, and later I am going to talk about one that you may have seen on that last day at Tulsa.

A key to playing good iron shots is to swing the club and don't try to hit the ball real hard. You are making a longer backswing with the longer irons and therefore you are creating more clubhead speed. On the longer irons take a wider stance, make a longer swing and the clubhead—right on until the follow-through is complete—does the work.

4
The Sand

I learned to play golf on a course in Nashville which is practically devoid of sand traps.

Yet, if I had to pinpoint one phase of my game which has been consistently sound throughout my tour career, it would be my play from bunkers. You have no doubt heard players say the sand shot is the easiest shot in golf, but it was not for me when I first went on tour. I worried about it more than any of my other strokes.

One morning I was fretting while working on my sand shots in a practice bunker in Napa, California. Phil Rodgers, a tour buddy of mine who has always been a strong sand player, was watching.

When he could stand it no longer, he came over to ask if I would like to hear his ideas about playing sand shots. Naturally I was ready to listen to anybody, but particularly to Phil because of his reputation as an outstanding sand player.

My problem was that I had a tendency to hit into the sand too close to the ball. Once that happens, once you hit the ball thin—"blade it," as we say—and it flies out too fast, too far, you become afraid of the shot. Anyone who has ever tried to play golf knows that this sort of apprehension, this sort of hesitancy—lack of confidence—will ruin you. My sand shots had me scared to death every time I walked into a trap.

A big part of my bad habit in the sand stemmed from letting up on the shot. When I was afraid, I would hit the ball thin and thus hit it too far. This caused me to quit on the sand shot. Consequently, I started coming up short on every one of them. Rodgers gave me the tip that I am now passing on to you.

On sand shots, those in traps at greenside, open the club face a little and put your weight slightly on the right foot and leg. Keep the weight there throughout the address and

19

With his stance slightly open—his left foot back from the intended line of flight—and the ball even with the left heel, Graham consciously keeps his weight on his right foot throughout the address and swing. (Photo by Jimmy Holt)

From the sand, Graham offers a significant suggestion which is demonstrated by the line drawn three to four inches back of the ball. With the sand wedge opened slightly, Graham plans to hit the sand at the line back of the ball. (Photo by Jimmy Holt)

swing. Do not shift the weight to the left side. From this position, when you hit into the sand the weight on your right side makes the club come back up. You don't dig into the sand, which almost always results in the ball being left right there in the trap while the club buries itself.

This tip has really made the big difference for me in sand shots. In looking back to Tulsa in the 1977 Open, my bunker play was probably the reason I remained in contention. I never had any problem with the sand, although the traps at Tulsa created quite a bit of controversy. New sand had been put in the traps in March before the Open in June. Most of the complaints had to do with the ball "plugging"—burying—when it landed in the bunkers on the fly. The pros said the sand was too new, too fluffy. However, my right side tip from Rodgers worked again, for I never had trouble getting the ball out of the sand.

THE SAND SHOT

Many players say they aim two inches back of the ball in the sand, but I aim three to four inches behind it. When I hit into the sand three or four inches back of the ball for an explosion shot, I find I never have to worry about blading the ball.

Naturally, when you hit this far back of the ball, you have to hit a little harder. Learning to swing harder gives you more confidence and makes you go on through the shot much better. Frankly, I believe you can spin the ball just as easily and bring the ball out just as softly by hitting four inches back of it as you can by hitting a couple of inches closer to the rear of the ball.

I have heard some players talking about playing a sand shot by pretending there is a string running perpendicularly from the top of the ball right on through its bottom. They say to hit the sand back of the ball and then try to take the sand wedge right on through and "cut" that imaginary string directly beneath the ball.

What they are really saying is to be sure you go on through the shot. If it takes this sort of imagination and concentration to play a sand shot, then use your imagination and concentrate! It can be the most important shot you develop.

Since Rodgers's lesson that day in California, I have refined my sand game by incorporating other tips too. For instance, after concentrating on setting up with my weight on the right side, I will envision trying to hit four inches back of the ball and knocking a divot of sand onto the green. This is another tip which, translated, means the good sand shots include a complete follow-through.

Playing sand shots is like having a good putting stroke. You will save many, many shots if you develop a good bunker game.

SAND CONDITIONS

I have had players ask me about the wiggling and twisting of my feet while taking my stance in a trap. Naturally, the idea here is to be sure you get your feet deep enough into the sand to make certain you do not shift or slip on the swing. Remember, you are going to hit deep into the sand and four inches behind the ball. This means you are going to be moving quite a bit of sand, so you must take a healthy swat at the ball. Make sure that you have your feet firmly planted.

There is another reason for this twisting of your feet into the sand in the trap. When I walk into a bunker, I want to get as much information as possible about the texture of the sand. The sand may look as though it is compacted, but is it really just crusty on top and loose underneath? The sand may appear dry, but is it wet an inch under the surface? Perhaps it looks wet on top, but is it dry beneath? Putting your feet in the sand helps determine the texture, plus get a feel for the sand.

All these conditions are very important

The flying sand shows how far back of the ball and line Graham's sand wedge struck. He is now attempting to knock an imaginary divot of sand onto the green as part of his explosion shot. (Photo by Jimmy Holt)

The dust has settled, and the crater-like bowl remains from Graham's sand shot, which began when he drove his sand wedge into the sand four inches back of the ball. Only now well after impact, has Graham shifted any weight from his right side to his left. (Photo by Jimmy Holt)

pieces of information. For instance, the wetter the sand, the harder you must swing to get the club through the shot if the sand is loose. If it is packed, wet sand, then hit it easy because the sand wedge will bounce and the ball will come out easier.

The Putter Alternative

I have been in traps where the sand looked heavy, but an inch down there was nothing but dirt. When this condition exists near the edge of the trap, and the ball is sitting high and dry on top of the sand, you might consider using your putter to get the ball onto the green. This rolling shot should never be attempted if there is any appreciable lip—overhang—on the trap.

If you do decide to putt the ball out of the trap, make absolutely certain you hit the ball with enough force to get it over the trap's lip. Strike it as though you are hitting a putt, but don't let the putter hit the sand first, and hit the ball solidly. Don't try to hit the ball with an upswing motion, for all this does is turn it down into the sand. I still prefer to blast 99 percent of the time.

The Buried Ball

If the ball should plug—bury—or gives the appearance of being a "fried egg" when it goes into a bunker, it will come out slower and the swing must be harder. Do not open the club face too much though. Just hit down and harder into the sand. Let the sharp edge (the leading edge) of the sand wedge go under the ball. On this type of shot, I usually move my target to about three inches back of the ball. The ball is played about in the middle of the stance, so you can hit down firmly and go deeper into the sand. Be sure to hit through the shot, and don't stop the club at the ball.

Remember, when the ball is buried it almost always is going to roll when it comes out of a trap. Try to adjust the strength of your blast shot for this anticipated roll. It is really very difficult to make a buried sand shot stop dead. Never try to "pick" the ball up from the sand.

If you open the club face, keep your weight on the right side, and try to knock a divot of sand onto the green, the ball is going to come out. The club face must never touch the ball on a sand wedge shot. It is the sand compacting behind the ball that forces the ball into the air and out of the trap.

Finally, I believe the main objective to keep in mind when playing a sand shot is to make certain your next shot is made with a putter. In other words, the idea of carrying a sand wedge is to use it once—only once—per trap. Get the ball out first, then worry about the putt.

5

The Putter

There is nothing, and I mean nothing, in golf that is as important as the putting stroke.

In the hands of a talented player, the putter has made a hero out of more than one golfer. In the hands of less-talented players, it has driven them away from the game.

The putter is the surest way to cover up other sins that may occur during the play of any round of golf. Generally speaking, a good putter is going to score well. I grew up putting in the moonlight on a green at a municipal course near my home in Nashville, and there is little doubt that the putter has been my most effective club.

PUTTER SELECTION

The selection of a putter is important. I prefer the mallet type because it looks good to me sitting back of the ball. I believe it also

is best for all types of grasses. When I was a youngster in Nashville I used a blade putter all the time, but every so often it would hang on the grass, so I switched.

Actually, you might think about getting your putter to match the grass at your club. In other words, find a putter you like and stick with it. I have always felt that confidence in putting is everything, and a lot of this confidence comes from being satisfied with your putter. Some players go through entire careers not using more than two or three putters.

There are times however when a change of putters may help. That time comes when you've absolutely lost all confidence in your putter. Switch, if this happens.

Before leaving your old club however, let me offer you a tip about changing putters. If you are down on your favorite putter, and it

As a youngster, Graham frequently practiced putting well past dinnertime, and he believes the putter is the most important club in the bag. Outstanding as a putter when he was a junior golfer in Tennessee, Graham then used a blade-type putter. He changed as a touring pro, because he feels the mallet-head style is more suited to the different grasses he must play on the PGA circuit. (Photo by John Bibb)

just doesn't seem to get the job done any more, go into the golf shop to the putter rack. Look them over and pick out what seems to you to be the worst looking putter there. Pick out one that you know you couldn't possibly use. Take it out to the putting green and work with it for four or five minutes. Then go over and pick up your own putter. You'll be amazed at how good the old putter looks sitting back of the ball. It might even give you renewed confidence in the club.

I have found this little change often works, and confidence, of course, is the name of the game when it comes to putting. You simply must believe in what you are doing when you are preparing to putt.

PUTTING

There are almost as many styles of putting stances and grips as there are putters. Some things though are basic to a good, solid putting stroke.

The Grip

Putting, first of all, is a completely different stroke from any we have discussed. Forget about the famous V in the chapter on the grip, or where the pressure points of the grip may be. Forget the placement of the thumbs, too, for I am convinced that anything that is comfortable and gets the job done is the putting grip for you.

I use what is called a reverse overlapping putter grip. That is, the forefinger of the left hand comes out over the top of the small and middle fingers of the right. The grip with the right hand is turned with the palm under the club more than on the regular iron or driver shot. It's not exactly underneath, but it is turned underneath so that the thumb points toward the hole a little bit. The left-hand palm also is under the club a bit. I feel that this eliminates the wrist cock and firms up the entire grip. It allows you to push the club back straighter, then push it through straighter. Thus, it becomes something of a pendulum stroke.

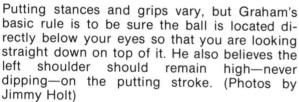

Putting stances and grips vary, but Graham's basic rule is to be sure the ball is located directly below your eyes so that you are looking straight down on top of it. He also believes the left shoulder should remain high—never dipping—on the putting stroke. (Photos by Jimmy Holt)

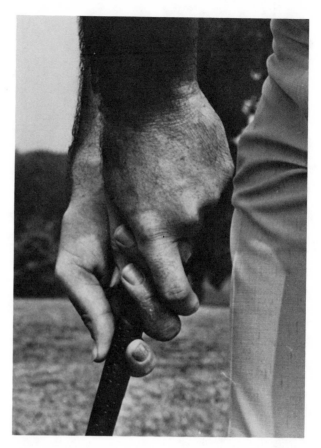

Graham uses the reverse overlapping putting grip. The grip with the right hand is turned underneath the shaft so that the right thumb is pointing a little toward the cup. The left forefinger comes over the top of the right little and ring fingers. The left thumb is on top of the shaft. Graham believes the putter should be gripped firmly, and he applies pressure with both thumbs.

I like to grip the putter firmly. Years ago when I was a wrist putter, I gripped lightly, very lightly, in order to improve the feel of my hands a little bit. Now I hold the putter very firmly, applying pressure with both thumbs. I press the putter with my thumbs more than any other part of my hands, although I do grip the club relatively firmly with the small fingers of my left hand.

Stance

My putting stance is a bit unusual because I wind up with my left elbow sticking straight out. It is almost pointing toward the hole. A lot of people have asked me if my elbow is really aiming at the cup.

It is not, as a matter of fact, aiming. Indeed, not until 10 or 12 years ago did I make this adjustment. It came after the late Dub Fondren, a professional in Memphis, worked with me to help cure my very wristy putting stroke. I had lost control of the wristy stroke, and Fondren decided I should cock my left wrist before the stroke began. This points my left elbow toward the cup, but it also gives a firmness in the wrist so that when I stroke

Early in his career, Graham utilized a wristy putting stroke which he demonstrates to show how his left wrist breaks on impact. It throws his left elbow toward the cup, and an alteration in his address has made his putting stance somewhat unusual.

through the ball, the wrists cannot cock again. They don't flip free, and it does away with the hinge in the wrists. So, I stick my left elbow out to eliminate this hingelike stroke.

Meanwhile, my right arm hangs away from the side. I do not hold it against my body and I don't push it out. It really is rather relaxed.

Like everything else in golf, I believe you have to keep your head still while putting. The length of the complete putting stroke varies from player to player, and putt to putt, but a good stroke will always be as long on the backswing as it is on the follow-through.

The ball is well away toward the hole and the putter has passed the left foot on the follow-through stroke, yet Graham's head remains motionless . . . until the putt is within inches of the cup. (Photos by Jimmy Holt)

Graham's left elbow points toward the cup because he is cocking his wrist before making his putting stroke. He believes this precocked wrist gives a firmness to his wrist so that when he strokes through the ball, the wrists do not cock again. His protuding left elbow eliminates the hinge in his wrists.

The ball should be placed directly below your eyes so that you are looking straight down on top of it. There are many good putters who don't use this rule, but that's because they have developed their own strokes without being taught. You may adjust this rule to fit your own style. Just remember, wherever you place your head, keep it still.

The Stroke

When I start my club back with the putter, I try to push it back with my left forearm. This is strictly my style, but it might work for you. With my left arm straight out, it is in great position to push the blade straight away

from the ball. This enables me to carry out another very basic procedure in putting: Keeping the putter blade low to the ground.

Also, no matter what grip or stance you use, your hands should be slightly ahead of the ball. They should remain there at impact. When you stroke back and then bring the putter forward to hit the ball, the hands still should be slightly ahead of the blade. This position prevents you from flipping the putter head at the ball. It really makes you pull the putter through, and this makes the ball roll much better.

Lining up a Putt

When lining up a putt, you should get behind the ball and look down the line of the putt. As you do this, you should visualize a line running from your ball into the cup. Then, follow the line and the imaginary ball as it runs along the green. It may take a break in one direction, run a few feet, then break in another direction as it turns toward the hole. Always follow this line right into the cup.

I get down behind a putt and look down the line and visualize the ball rolling until it gets to the cup. Maybe it's a little too high above the hole, so I go through the imaginary ball-rolling process again, until I "see" it go right into the cup.

The Long Putt

Let's take the long approach putt first, for it is most important in preventing the worst enemy on the greens—the three-putt.

I often hear amateur players say, "Well, I didn't leave it short," after they have run an approach putt five feet past the cup. I never believe in charging any putt. I think a good putt is the putt that rolls right up to the cup and, if it misses, goes maybe six to eight inches past the hole. This sort of putting is especially important in tournament play because you don't have any "gimmies." You always have to make the next one. Nobody is

going to give you that one- or two-footer. So your best approach putt is the one that goes by the cup six to eight inches.

Always line up your shot and try to roll the long putt with enough speed so that if the ball touches any part of the cup it will drop in. That is the perfect speed.

The Short Putt

On the short putts, those three- and four-footers, I am concerned first with the grain in the green. If the green is grainy and I am against the grain or cross-grain, then I like to try to drive the ball into the hole. That way, it doesn't bounce around and get off line.

On a slick green, when I'm going with the grain, I like to hit the putt that is traveling just fast enough that the cup seems to reach out and grab the ball if it gets near. It is just a smooth, dying sort of putt with little speed. On a three-foot putt, a good putt is one that stops four inches past if it doesn't drop. Certainly, a three-footer should never be more than five inches past.

READING THE GREEN

After you walk up on the green and you are waiting for your partner to putt, take the time to study your own putt. Then when it is your turn, you will be ready to step up and putt. This concentration should help you get yourself "pumped up" to make the putt.

Nothing in golf requires more concentration and total involvement than putting. You have to become completely engrossed in what's happening. You must be able to read a green, and this involves figuring out the grain, the slopes, and the speed of the grass.

These phases of putting are as important as the stroke you have worked on. If you can't read the green, then no matter how good your stroke is, you can't make the putt consistently.

The Grain

People often tell me they can't really see

the grain in a green, but it isn't that difficult to determine. When you are looking at the dark part of the green you are looking into the grain, and when you are looking at the bright—lighter—color you are looking down-grain. The lighter color is caused by the sun reflecting off the back of the grass. The shadows underneath the grass create the darker shade. Down-grain the speed of the green is fast, and the speed is slower when you putt against the grain. When the ball is dying somewhere near the cup, you should be absolutely certain of the direction of the grain. The grain can make or break a fine putt.

By learning to distinguish between these colors, you will improve your putting. If you want to learn these color distinctions, go to the practice putting green and walk slowly in a circle. You will see the change in color as you circle.

Slopes

A break, the slope in a green, depends on the speed of the putt. The harder you hit the ball, the less break you must play. However, if you will learn to play each putt so that it stops no more than six or eight inches past the cup—if it doesn't drop—then you will soon learn to read all breaks about the same. That's because the speed of your putts is going to become consistent.

On a very slick green you must play more break, because the speed of your putt will allow the ball to turn more. Slower greens will have less breaks because the ball is hit harder and rides down in the grass as it goes along. The slick green allows the ball to ride right on top and takes extremely big breaks. Some very slick greens won't have much grain either.

Speed of the Grass

I think a good thing for a lot of club members to work on is getting used to slow greens. Most club greens are slower than those we play on the tour. I have found that when you get on very slow greens, if you hold your putter up so that it barely touches the grass you can take a longer backswing much easier. By holding the club so it just touches the grass, you swing more freely with the pendulum and there is little danger of dragging the putter on the grass.

Actually, I have found a little tip that I use on fast greens, too. Just before the U.S. Open at Winged Foot in 1974, I discovered that if I never grounded my putter—if I never let it touch the green at any time during address, backswing, or stroke—I could control the length of the stroke and thus the speed of the putt much better. Open greens usually are lightning fast, and since Winged Foot, I've been very fortunate in this championship. [Graham was third in 1974, first in 1975, and second in 1977].

Keeping the club off the ground all the time isn't unique with me. Watch Jack Nicklaus. In some tournaments, he does it with all his clubs, not just the putter.

PUTTING PRACTICE

Practice putting may be the most fun of all golf work, and I am sure it is the most rewarding. It may be carried out almost anywhere. For instance, the leg of your coffee table in the den makes a fine target. When practicing, though, always play a game in your mind—pretend you have to make this putt to win the Masters, just to make each putt seem important.

Perhaps my best tip for practice putting is one I remember from an article by Horton Smith that I read 20 years ago. I have used this tip time and again, and I've passed it along to others who also find it really helps them.

I take a golf ball and put it in my left hand, in the small fingers of my left hand, underneath the edge of the grip. I putt with my regular grip, holding the ball under the shaft. I hit four or five putts, and then I go back to the normal grip without the ball. This gives

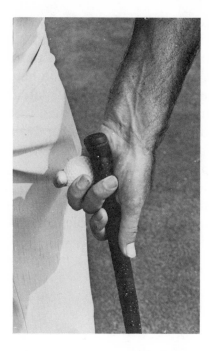

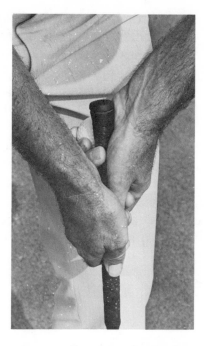

For a practice putting tip, Graham begins by placing a golf ball in the small fingers of his left hand.

He puts the ball under the edge of the putter grip, squeezing the ball tightly with his left little fingers.

Placing his right hand into putting position, Graham keeps the ball in his left hand snug against the putter girp.

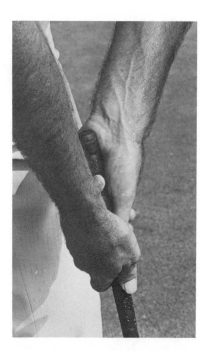

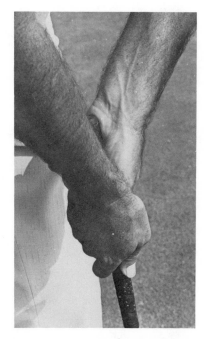

Closing the grip in a "normal" fashion, Graham hits four or five practice putts while holding the golf ball in his left fingers under the shaft of the putter. Graham says when the ball is removed he has considerably more touch in the putting stroke with his left hand. (Photos by Jimmy Holt)

me a little bit more of a touch feeling in my left hand. Somehow, I begin to get control of the clubhead, getting a feel that runs from my hands right down the shaft. I just have to hit four or five putts this way and I am always amazed at how it helps me begin to feel the left hand control the putter blade.

Usually, after spending considerable time on a putting green working on your putting, you tend to stiffen. Your back gets tired, you may lose concentration, and you begin to lose the feel of your stroke. Under these circumstances, a good way to regain your natural stroke is to drop a ball and putt across the green five or six times, not even putting toward the hole or with any specific distance in mind. Just putt the ball. Stroke the ball, maybe even drop a couple of balls and putt at them with your eyes closed. You'll find that your natural putting stroke, your natural feel of the putter, begins to return.

My final tip on putting involves the left shoulder, or the shoulder facing the cup. I have found that by keeping it high, never letting it dip toward the hole, I am able to maintain the pendulum stroke.

6
The Driver

If the putter is the most important club in the bag, the driver is not far behind.

Routinely, a player will start 14 of 18 holes by using his driver, and where the drive comes to rest sets up the strategy and play. So, before getting into what I consider to be the stroke-savers in the driving phase of golf, let me make one simple, but frequently overlooked, observation:

Don't just walk onto the tee, set up your golf ball, and drive. Aim the ball somewhere. Spend a second or two concentrating on a target, or at least a general area of where you'd like to see the ball stop.

This may sound a bit foolish, but I've played with many a partner in pro-amateurs and other events who simply never takes the time to aim on the drive. Pick out a tree, a bush, a rain shelter, water fountain—anything—as a target and then try to hit the ball toward it. Some of the most unusual golf shots I've ever seen come from drives on what I consider wide-open holes. The player just doesn't take that second or two to see where he wants to hit his drive in order to set up the play of the hole. The results of such a lack of concentration are amazing. You see hooks, slices, tops, and fat shots due to merely teeing it up and taking a swat at it.

DRIVER SELECTION

The selection of a driver is as important, I believe, as the selection of a putter. Most players purchase their woods in matched sets, and in making your selection, I think the emphasis should be on the No. 1 wood in the set. That, of course, is the driver.

The majority of players I know use a driver with a 43-inch shaft. They use the R, or regular, stiffness in the shaft. The other stiff,

Because of his low-key personality and his willingness to help amateur partners, Graham is in great demand in pro-am and executive-type golf events. Graham's partner in one of the early Music City USA Pro-Celebrity tournaments in Nashville was Lawrence Welk. (Photo by Joe Rudis)

or flex, ratings are the S for stiff and X for the extra stiff or strong shaft. I feel a swing weight of D-3 is good for most of the amateurs I see around the country at the various pro-ams. By comparison, I use a 43¼-inch driver with an X-shaft and a swing weight of D-2½. This means my driver is a little bit stronger than what I consider a regular amateur's club.

TEEING UP THE BALL

As I have already mentioned, much of the trouble that comes from poor driving stems

from such oversights as forgetting to aim. I've watched amateur players on tees where they give little, if any, consideration to the simple—but absolutely vital—process of teeing up the ball.

The ball should be teed at the same height each time, unless there is some weather factor that mandates an alteration in the height of the ball. For example, when you are hitting into the wind and you want the ball to bore into the wind, you might tee it just a tiny bit lower than usual. Conversely, if there is a nice strong wind back of you and you want to

A big part of setting up a shot is to spend a moment concentrating on a target. Here, with long-time golfing & business associate Lou King, Graham studies the hole and the premier landing area for his drive. (Photo by Jimmy Holt)

get the ball flying high, then tee it a bit higher and play the ball maybe a little farther forward in your stance.

I know some golfers who claim they can tilt the tee forward a bit and get extra roll on their drives. I've tried it—not recently—and it never really worked with any consistency for me. I'm not knocking the tilt idea, you understand. It just doesn't work every time, at least not for me.

Here is how I get the ball teed at the same height for each drive. I put the tee between my middle finger and forefinger and my thumb on top of the ball. I press down on the ball and tee with the thumb until the tops of the two fingers touch the ground. Then, I back up the tee and ball just slightly, until I can't feel the ground. Such a setup is the perfect height for me, for it leaves half the ball to show above the club face. That is the ideal driving height.

Another thing that happens when you back the tee up a wee bit is that the tee is not stuck hard-and-fast in the ground. Most of the time it will fly loose—rather than break—when you drive. I've had amateur partners say that

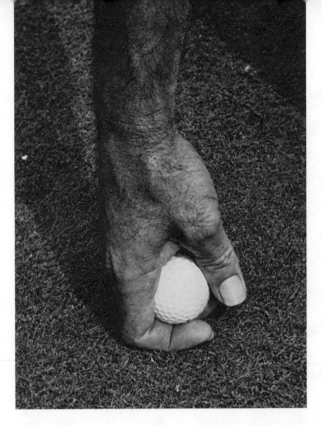

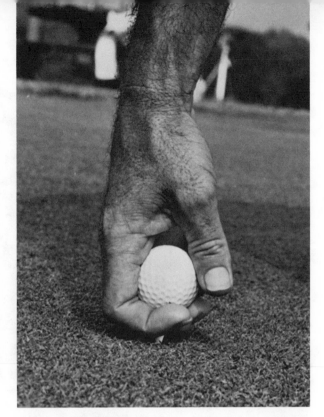

According to Graham, players should develop a routine for teeing the ball so as to maintain a consistency in the height of the ball at address. His routine is to insert the tee until the tops of his two fingers touch the ground.

After inserting the tee deep enough for the tops of his fingers to feel the ground, Graham backs the tee and ball off slightly until he no longer feels the ground. This is the perfect height for him.

The ideal driving height, unless there is a wind factor, is to have the ball showing half above the club face. Graham also prefers to have the trademark at the rear of the ball to offer a target as well as to improve his concentration on the stroke.

this is a great idea of how to tee up but, "at my club the tees are so hard in the summer I have to drive the peg into the ground with a driver. What can I do about that?" My answer is to change courses.

I always position the ball on the wooden tee with the trademark toward the rear. In other words, the name of the ball will be against the club face on impact. This is not just a habit. There are definite reasons for this pattern of teeing up.

For one thing, having the trademark at the rear gives me a little something extra to concentrate on as I prepare to strike the ball. As I look at the ball, I can see the writing and I concentrate on hitting the ball in the rear.

With a driver, you hit sort of a sweeping stroke, sweeping the ball off the tee. So you are really looking at the back part of the ball, for that is where you will strike it. With middle and short irons, of course, you hit down

On the address of the driver, Graham suggests positioning the hands slightly back of the ball. This is because the driver shot is a sweeping-like swing that imparts top-spin on the ball. (Photo by Jimmy Holt)

and through the ball, so you are really looking at the top of the ball. Putting the trademark at the rear, then, should help you concentrate on the hitting area and the sweep-type stroke.

THE ADDRESS

For the address of the driver, I like to get my hands slightly behind the ball, while on the address of irons the hands are slightly ahead of the ball. This is because the driver shot is a sweeping-type swing, and irons are hit down and into the ball in order to put

backspin on the shot. Fairway woods also require the sweeping-type shot, so again the hands at address for them should be even with or slightly behind the ball.

As you may see, some of these driving tips are not what you might call your basic fundamentals of golf. However, I believe them to be tips which will help you improve your scoring, and that's what everybody wants to do—save a shot or two every round.

When taking your driver stance you move in the same way as if you were hitting your irons. Place your right foot forward and

Shoulder-width distance is required for the driver, fairway woods, and long irons. The weight distribution at address must be between the balls of your feet and back toward the heels a little bit. The right knee presses toward the left, and the left presses slightly inward. This prevents wobble during the swing. (Photos by Jimmy Holt)

place the clubhead back of the ball. The right foot should be square with the intended line of play.

Now, bring the left foot forward with the toe turned slightly to the left. As a matter of fact, the left toe on all shots—woods, irons, and especially chips—is turned left. This allows you to move through the shot, your left side can get out of the way, and you finish your swing well over on the left side of the left foot.

Occasionally, I'll have people ask me why it is that I can get so much more distance on my drive than they do. One big reason is because when they finish their swing they are over on the left side, but flat on their left foot. If you look at the long hitters in golf, amateurs or pros, you see that when they finish their swings, their weight is on the outside of their left foot. Rolling your weight up on the outer edge of the left foot, allows you to hit through and complete the shot with all the weight distributed properly at impact.

Watch a long hitter such as Jim Dent and see how as he drives through the ball, his legs drive through and his weight shifts and rolls in so hard that it goes on to the outside of the left foot. I believe this weight-shift and roll-up on the left foot are the most difficult part of driving for the average player.

Many of Lou Graham's Mondays are devoted to lectures and golf clinics. His easy-to-understand tips and demonstrations are helping him add the reputation as a teacher to this credentials as a championship player. Here Graham describes Jim Dent's powerful driving stroke. Graham directs attention to Dent's finish, "where Dent's weight has shifted to the outer edge of his left foot. I believe this weight-shift and roll-up on the left foot is the most difficult part of driving for the average player." (Photo by Dan Loftin)

The stance on the drive should be shoulder width. If you took a yardstick and measured the width of your shoulders and then placed that measurement between your heels, this would be a good rule for the proper distance between your feet for a good stance. It should never be any wider, but may be adjusted to a narrower stance.

In addressing the ball, your weight should be distributed between the balls of your feet and back toward the heels a little bit. There is slightly more weight on the inside of your right foot which allows you to press the right knee toward the left knee. The left knee also is pressed slightly inward, and this position will allow the knees to work toward one another and not wobble forward or backward during the swing.

(Above Left) Throughout the swing, except on the finish, the knees are flexed, the right knee tucked toward the left on address and held tucked slightly.

(Above) The weight on the inside of your right foot allows you to press the right knee toward the left knee.

(Left) The left knee also is pressed slightly inward, and this position allows the knees to work toward one another and not wobble forward or backward during the swing. (Photos by Jimmy Holt)

THE BACKSWING

At all times throughout the swing—except on the finish—the knees are flexed, the right knee tucked toward the left on address and held tucked slightly throughout. You will find this makes you swing the club back straighter, makes the clubhead go up on the backswing rather than inside real fast. If the

As the strength builds at the top of the backswing, there should be a taut feeling in the left arm and left side as though it wants automatically to pull down into the ball. The pull down is at the grip end of the club, back toward the ball. It all comes down in a one-piece motion and on until the follow-through is complete. (Photos by Jimmy Holt)

right knee is allowed to go back too far and straighten out, it allows the right hip to turn and the club is pulled back away from the ball too much on the inside of the swing. The right knee stays tucked and holds the hip in position to restrict the backswing so that it doesn't go back too far. It gives you the feeling of building strength at the top of the swing, like a rubber band being stretched.

When you get to the top of the backswing, there should be a taut feeling in the left arm and left side, as though it wants automatically to pull back down into the ball. If the right knee straightens out, you kill this elastic-type feeling on the left side and that results in an incorrect transfer of weight and

power, causing poor control and hooks, slices, tops, and bloops.

But, if the left toe remains turned slightly toward the target, and the right knee stays tucked, you will get this spring-back sensation which makes you return the club properly and on a true line back into the ball. It also produces extra distance, for you have everything coming back at once, rather than trying to force it back.

At the top of the backswing the left forearm and the left wrist should be in a straight line. In other words, if you put a board along the edge of your forearm and wrist, the board would be flat across both. Sometimes you see a golfer get to the top of the swing with the

(Above) As the backswing develops on the drive, the left heel begins to break loose from the ground as the weight begins to move toward the inside of the left foot.

(Below) The higher the backswing goes, the higher the outside of the left heel lifts until at the top of the swing the outer edge of the left heel comes up perhaps and inch and a half or two inches.

(Above) As the downswing begins, the weight begins to shift toward the outside of the left foot.

(Below) At the completion of the swing, the weight transfer is complete, and now the right heel has come off the ground and the weight has gone to the left side, actually to the outer left side of the left foot. (Photos by Jimmy Holt)

wrist cocked toward the forearm. It causes a crease where you can actually see the roll of skin crinkling in the wrist. This is wrong. There should never be any roll of skin across or around the wrist. It should be smooth, indicating the wrist and forearm are in a straight line, parallel to the ground.

The wrist should not break the other way, allowing the clubhead to fall toward the ground. This causes you to lose control at the top and puts a tremendous strain on the forearm. When your left wrist and forearm are straight at the top, you can feel yourself pulling the end of the club—the grip end—back toward the ball. It's all coming down in a one-piece motion.

THE DOWN SWING

At the top of the backswing on a driver shot, the left heel comes off the ground—just slightly—rolling the weight toward the inside of the left foot. The left outer edge of the left heel comes up perhaps an inch and a half or two inches. This same foot action occurs on long iron shots. On short irons, I think the heel should stay on the ground, giving you better stability and helping you hit the ball straighter. On short irons, of course, the idea is *accuracy* as opposed to distance. So you take a shorter swing and keep the heel on the ground.

The downswing starts with the left arm and shoulder pulling the grip. You don't push it out and throw the clubhead at the ball with your hands. You *pull* it back down, *pulling* the *grip* end first! When you start to pull the

grip back down, the left heel returns to the ground and you begin to shift the weight toward the outside of the left foot. At the completion of the swing, the right heel is off the ground, the weight having gone to the left side.

I like to spend time now and then watching fellow touring pros on the practice tee. If you go to a tournament, watch the players practice. Watch them swing, and then shut your eyes and visualize the swing in your mind. Try to get the rhythmic movement they have. When I feel I am not swinging well, I will go and watch Gene Littler practice. I watch other pros too, but I prefer to watch Littler and to try to remember what I saw, especially his rhythm.

I don't try to duplicate Littler's swing; I don't think anybody could do that. But the tempo, the rhythm of his swing, is tremendous. It is like a rocking chair swing, back and forth, effortless. He never consciously tries to force speed into the swing. Yet, the speed builds up, like a rocking chair. He takes the club back, pauses, then builds speed through impact and on into the follow-through. Try to get this rhythm, this rocking chair effect, in mind.

This is important because if you are out on the course playing and you are having trouble with your game, take a second, maybe while waiting for somebody else to shoot. Just close your eyes and picture this swing in your mind. It's the consistent, smooth motion you want. It's the sort of alteration that can help you recover your game, right there during a round.

7

The Wedge

After the putter and driver, the third most important club in the bag is the wedge.

When I talk about the wedge, I'm really referring to the sand iron, for not only is it used in the bunkers, but I use it from 90 to 100 yards out. In most cases, I believe just about every pro follows this same plan.

It is very difficult to find a sand wedge that is properly fitted for an individual player. So many clubs are not made exactly as you want them to be, and I think this is true for the amateur as well as the tour pro.

The difference seems to be the fact that once a pro finds a club that feels pretty good to him and looks good sitting back of the ball, he begins to add a twist here, a little weight there. Almost every wedge on tour has been filed some way in order to alter the sole of the club so it will meet the individual pro's personal specification.

For this reason, I believe every amateur should carry both a pitching wedge and a sand wedge. It also is a very good idea for a player to learn as closely as possible just how far he is able to hit a pitching wedge. This is because so many wedge shots are recovery shots that may lead to one-putt pars, or they offer the player a golden opportunity for a birdie.

The point here is that if a person knows almost to the inch how far he can hit the wedge, the shot then can become almost as useful—with practice and accuracy, of course—as an approach putt.

I am a big believer in using less-lofted clubs such as the 5-6-7-8-9 irons for those delicate little chips and flips around the greens. Few pros, for example, use their wedges for chips right at the edge of the putting surface. When they get that close, say in

The sand wedge is an excellent club for playing from deep, fluffy areas because it cuts through the grass and doesn't grab like a wedge or 9-iron. There is no reason for a wide stance, because there is no great distance or strength required. Graham keeps his feet closer together than on any other shot and his feet point in the general direction of the cup. (Photos by Jimmy Holt)

To regain the feel of the stroke-saving chip and short wedge shots, Graham recommends tossing golf balls underhand toward the cup or a bucket in the yard at home. The action is similar to the chip shot stroke, and Graham calls particular attention to the position of the feet. He believes they should be, as in this photograph, pointing toward the target on chip shots. (Photo by Jimmy Holt)

short grass and four or five feet off the putting surface, they chip with the 7-8-9. I like to play the 9-iron a great deal on this type of chip.

I use my sand wedge out of the deep, fluffy sort of collars on greens that we run into sometimes, because the sand wedge cuts through the grass. It doesn't hang up in the grass like a pitching wedge or 9-iron. The ball pops up onto the green very easily.

On any chip shot I use a very open stance, with the feet closer together than at any other time. Actually, both feet are pointing in the general direction of the cup. I have a little tip to go along with this sort of stance.

When you are losing the feel of the chip shot, go to a green and practice a bit by taking a half-dozen golf balls and tossing them underhand toward the cup. Just see how close you are able to pitch and roll the ball to the hole. The stance you take is similar to that of a softball pitcher. If no green is handy, try tossing the balls into a bucket in the back yard.

While you're tossing toward the cup, stop and look at the position of your feet. Notice they are pointing toward the target—the cup. That's what I believe should be the position of your feet when you are chipping. There's no reason for a wide, strong stance because distance is immaterial. The effort on the chip shot is to get the ball as close as possible to the pin, so you can save a stroke by one-putting.

Properly executed, the wedge shot can be the most satisfying in golf. It is a relatively difficult club to learn to use because it combines some of each of the two swings in the game—the golfing stroke and the putting stroke. Once a player gains confidence in his wedge play, he begins to get the ball closer on the chips and short shots, and this style of play strengthens his entire game and saves a lot of strokes.

Properly executed, the wedge shots from right around the edges of the greens can be the most satisfying in golf. The shot combines parts of putting and the golfing stroke and the wrists are cocked just as the club head reaches knee height. It is one of the more difficult strokes to master, but once you learn it, it is a real shot-saver.

8
Use 'em All

One of the more amusing aspects of golf is to watch the player whose ego is such that he simply cannot bring himself to hit more club than the others in his foursome. This golfer gets a special kick out of being able to leave both feet, pull a back muscle, and blister both hands while hitting a sand wedge 180 yards.

"Thought I might not have enough club," the player will say while placing the wedge back in the bag after making sure that all the 3- and 4-iron shooters in the group are aware he hit the wedge.

Such strong golfers are doomed. They never will understand the finesse of golf, and never will establish any continuity in their games. They are doomed until they realize it is no disgrace to use all 14 clubs.

In researching for this book, I discovered an interesting fact that I plan to use in later chapters to help you understand how all the information and tips go into an actual round of golf. I found that on my last round of the Open at Tulsa, when I made a pretty good run at Hubert Green, I used every club in my bag in shooting a 68.

The point is that the rules allow you to carry 14 clubs, so why not make use of them when the need arises. It's okay, I suppose, to hit a 7-iron "light" when a good, full 8-iron is the club, but my advice is to use the lesser club and hit it hard.

I have always felt that if you need a 4-iron, hit it. Don't be squeamish about hitting more club than everybody else on the tee. Also, I feel it is usually better for the amateur player to use the lesser club on those devilish, in-between shots. I mean those shots, for example, when you can't decide whether to use a 4- or 5-iron.

Take the weaker club and hit it firmly rather than attempting the stronger club and hitting it easier. I really don't recommend easing

It usually is much better to use a lesser club and hit it firm than to take the smaller club and hit it easy. On those "in between" shots, then, Graham says if you can't decide on a 4 or 5 iron, take the 5 iron and hit it full. (Photo by Jimmy Holt)

off any shot. True, a slow, controlled swing is important, but the hesitant, hit-it-lightly swinger has too many opportunities to get the club off track.

If you take the longer club and try to choke it down and take a little off the shot, you are going to wind up easing into the shot and hanging the ball to the right, or coming over the top and going left. You can do just about anything in this situation. When you ease off, you will find a great number of your shots are hit "fat" because you are not going at them with full confidence.

When you take the lesser club and swing hard, be sure to complete your backswing.

Get the club all the way back until you can get a good pause at the top before beginning to pull the club back through the ball.

If you try to hit a club hard and start hitting at it from the very beginning of your swing, you bring the club back too fast, lose your timing and tempo, make mistakes, and lose your strokes.

CLUB SELECTION

Club selection is extremely important at any level of golf. At the PGA tour level you will see and hear players talking in terms of yards and feet, and few pros vary more than 10 yards from one club to another. I can tell within 5 to 10 yards exactly how far I can hit each club in my bag. This is absolutely required information for those of us playing different golf courses each week.

I believe it is vital too for the club member to know—as closely as possible—exactly how far he hits each of his clubs, even though he plays the same course week after week.

Nothing is more distracting than to be standing over the ball and be undecided as to whether you are holding the proper club. There already is far too much distraction in this game. For the good player, indecision is the cause of more missed shots than anything. Learn how far you can hit each club!

Learn through Practice

The best way to learn your distances is to go to the practice tee and hit some shots. Then mark off the distance of what you think is your best shot with each club, and figure your average distances. Now, go to the course by yourself and hit various clubs to the greens so you learn exactly how far you can carry the ball. Pace out from the green so you know your distance.

Factors that Influence Club Selection

A player should keep in mind that conditions other than weather often affect a shot. There are times when the match is tight or you have a super round going and you get all "pumped up." Suddenly, instead of hitting a 5-iron 150 yards, you are hitting it 160 yards. It is important to recognize this feeling, for club selection may change under such circumstances. If you do not adjust, you may spoil your round because you suddenly are "hitting it too well."

Another thing to keep in mind about club selection is that all golf sticks are not alike. In other words, my 5-iron isn't likely to be the same as yours. Because I practice and play almost every day, I have filed, refined, bent, and twisted most of my clubs so they are suited as perfectly as possible to my needs and my game.

Instead of adjusting the physical properties of your clubs, you may find it better to make certain mental alterations. For instance, your 5-iron may not be as strong as somebody else's, and another player's wedge may be weaker than yours. Club selection becomes an absolutely individual process, and may change from one set of clubs to another.

I strongly urge players to visit their professional when purchasing golf clubs. The clubs you buy in a pro shop are the same as those used by the tour players, and the club pro is well qualified to suggest lengths, weights, and lofts. The extra time and money spent in seeking a pro's advice is well worthwhile.

For the record, here are the distances for my clubs:

Driver—245 yards and up
3-wood—230-245 yards
4-wood—215-230 yards
2-iron—200-215 yards
3-iron—190-200 yards
4-iron—180-190 yards
5-iron—170-180 yards
6-iron—160-170 yards
7-iron—150-160 yards
8-iron—140-150 yards
9-iron—120-140 yards
Pitching wedge—100-120 yards
Sand wedge—100 yards and under

Many tour pros carry a 1-iron, but I do not. I prefer a 4-wood because I believe there are more occasions to use a 4-wood than a 1-iron. Besides, I think the 4-wood is an easier club to hit.

9

The Thinking Game

Earlier, I indicated that the putter and wedges may be the best stroke-savers in *golf*. I would like to amend that appraisal by saying that those clubs are the best stroke-savers in the *bag*. The surest stroke-saver of all is located in the area between each player's ears.

Thinking a round of golf is as important to the score as hitting the shots. The ability to avoid the double bogey may be the biggest challenge for any medium or high handicap player. I venture to say that just about every 85 shooter you know has at least two doubles on every card. When the day comes that the 85 shooter eliminates those doubles, he's going to be moving toward the 70s, and for most amateurs that is truly a milestone in the game.

PLAN YOUR NEXT SHOT

One of the bits of know-how which made

the late Bobby Jones such a great master of golf was his constant attention to the next shot. People who knew him as a player say Jones was always planning, always thinking. He played very quickly, I'm told, because as he walked toward his ball after hitting one shot, he approached the ball on the line of intended flight for the next shot. This sort of approach had to give him a great overall picture of what his next shot should be, and it enabled him to establish a tempo which was rarely interrupted by having to walk ahead to see where to play a shot.

When planning the next shot, I always try to be sure to look and see what will happen to the ball if the shot isn't hit exactly as I want. This sort of managing will be of great help to you in avoiding the double and triple bogies. You may recover from bogies, but the doubles and triples take a lot of playing to get back. If you get two or three of them, an 18-

hole round doesn't last long enough for you to recover from them.

Examine the Greens

Walking behind the intended line of flight for the next shot has many advantages, not the least of which is keeping your mind on what you are trying to do on the round. Even such subtle observations as the roll in the greens, which gives you an overall picture of the putting surface, can be most valuable.

For the regular club member the overall picture of a green may not be too important, because after a few rounds most of us know the general breaks and undulations in the greens. However, when you are playing on strange greens or away from your home course, there are times when it is difficult to determine such basic things as whether a putt is uphill or downhill.

I have been places where a member of the foursome—a touring pro, mind you—has said, "Gosh, I thought that putt was downhill. No wonder I came up eight feet short." I have had the same sensation.

In order to be sure of having the correct rolls and breaks and directions in mind, pros will walk on both sides of the cup and view the green from all angles. This too is why I think it is extremely valuable to follow your shots by planning the next and going along the intended line of play as you approach the ball.

Wind Variations

Another playing tip that I have found to be valuable in altering my game as I play is to observe the wind at the tops of trees. Most of us tell the wind direction and velocity from the flag on the green, but many times a shot goes up above the trees into winds there. The direction and speed of the winds above the trees also has to be considered in selecting clubs. Often the winds up above are more important than those at the green. Be sure you plan the shot with all weather elements in mind.

Graham feels many of the problems created in a golf swing come from head movement. To help keep the head still, Graham suggests bringing the left shoulder up under the chin on the backswing. This keeps everything solid and allows Graham to get a full backswing too. (Photo by Jimmy Holt)

HEAD CONTROL

Everybody who ever picked up a golf club has heard the expression "Keep your head down." I think maybe a better, more readily understood tip might be to say "Keep your head still."

A great deal of the real problems created in a golf swing come from head movement. This is true in putting, too. Some players like to stare at the ball in an effort to keep from moving their heads. That may be okay for them, but I don't recommend it. If I try to stare at the ball while hitting it, I begin to tighten up, so I take a good, concentrated look, but I don't stare.

When hitting any shot, the idea is to concentrate, but don't stare. This helps keep the head still which is vital to a good swing. Graham believes when he brings his left shoulder right up under his chin on the backswing this keeps things solid and helps him get the full backswing, too.

One way I manage to keep my head still is to bring my left shoulder right up under my chin on the backswing. This keeps everything pretty solid, and helps me get a full backswing, too.

BE READY TO ADJUST

I don't mind making adjustments or alterations while I am playing a round, even a tournament round. As a matter of fact, later we'll talk about how I actually made a change during the last day of the Open in Tulsa. That adjustment put me right back in contention.

Some golfers will say, "Oh, don't try to change while you're playing. Wait till you get on the practice tee." I disagree. A lot of players never get a chance to get to the practice tee for one thing, and adjustments can be made that aren't drastic enough to warrant a lot of practice tee work.

Use the Sun

One of my favorite tips for players to get an overall picture of what they are doing, maybe even what they are doing wrong, is limited to the position of the sun. That's right. The sun.

Late in the afternoon your body casts a pretty good shadow. When you are having problems, walk along and swing the club and take a look at your shadow. It's like watching an instant replay. You can check the height and position of your hands at the top of the swing. You can watch your leg and knee action. You can watch the position of your head and the extent of your body and/or shoulder turn.

I have found this shadow idea to be most valuable. The only trouble is, of course, you can't do much shadow-looking at noon, if that happens to be your starting or playing time.

Graham utilizes the sun and his shadow to create a do-it-yourself instant replay effect. He uses the shadow to check the height and position of hands at the top of the swing, the leg and knee action, and the extent of body and shoulder turn. (Photo by Jimmy Holt)

THINK AS YOU PLAY

Playing and saving strokes are the name of the game most days. Sometimes you can go out and play a round and not play well at all, but if you *think* and pay attention to what you are doing, you will save shots. When you get into trouble and think about all the alternatives and decide which one you want to attempt, you should take your time and visualize exactly what you want to try. That's when you really begin to save the shots.

On the other hand, if you go out there and just go blank and get upset because of the way things are going, then you are in for a

The legs provide tremendous strength to the swing and shot. As the weight shifts from right to left, the pulling down on the backswing is all in one piece right on through the transfer of the weight to the outside of the left foot. (Photos by Jimmy Holt)

long day. You'll lose and waste a bunch of strokes with such an attitude.

While playing golf, you always have to stop and think about what's going on, how you want to play a shot, and what is going to happen if you don't hit it just right. Where will the ball go? Will you wind up in double-bogey position? Or, will you be in a position where you can still get away with par?

That's the name of the game—being able to score.

When you come in off the course and the other golfers are sitting around in the locker room, they want to know one thing: What did you shoot? They don't really want to know whether you took a fast backswing or a short backswing, and they don't want to know what club you hit. They just want to know what you shot. I think players who spend the round concentrating on what they're doing and thinking as they go are going to be able to report a lower score than those who spend the afternoon fretting and fussing about hitting a bad shot or missing a putt.

10
The Trouble Shot

None of us hits the ball straight every time. Let me hit it straight on every shot, and I'll be right around the top of the prize list every Sunday night!

Patience is the key to making successful recovery shots after the one you tried to hit straight went wrong. Red-hot scoring rounds aren't created, they just happen. They won't happen, though, if you misplay recovery shots, or if you misplan them.

Furthermore, if you hit a bad shot or you get a bad break, don't waste your time worrying and pouting about what might have happened. Put all your concentration and patience into the next shot.

You simply have to get totally involved in the game. I have shot some of my better scores when I wasn't playing very well. I had the good scoring round because I worked and concentrated every second I was on the course.

Then when I finished the round, I could look back and say, "Boy, that was fun out there today, not because I hit the ball so well, but because I didn't let anything other than playing golf enter my mind."

Staying busy mentally often enables players to stay out of trouble and more importantly, perhaps, helps them solve their problems once the poor shots occur.

RECOVERY AT MEDINAH

I have hit my share of poor shots, and the strange thing is that two of them—one in Chicago and one in Tulsa—probably led to more affirmative publicity for me than many of the good shots I have hit.

The poor shot at Tulsa, in the last round of the Open, led to the widely shown escape from the trees at the 17th hole. The one in Chicago came on the last hole of the play-off against John Mahaffey for the U.S. Open Championship in 1975. It was a bad 2-iron shot—actually, I hit it straight, but too far—that led to a recovery shot that really won the championship.

The thinking behind the recovery shot in Chicago at Medinah helped me win the most prestigious golf championship in the world. But, actually the trouble shot was no different than most every golfer encounters when facing decisions before attempting recovery strokes.

I made the shot successfully because I believe there are certain rules that must be followed before, during, and after trouble shots.

I made my recovery at Medinah with a 4-iron, which was not your ordinary, two-bit Nassau gamble. This boy was for real. I knew if I pulled it off, I would win the big one, because at the time I decided to try the shot, I was leading Mahaffey by two strokes. He was in the middle of the fairway with a 5-iron in his hands. He knew that if I messed this thing up in the trees, he had a chance to get it all right there on the last hole.

Remember a few pages ago when we were talking about how the toughest shot is the one that you have to hit straight? Well, I got myself into the mess at Medinah by trying to *avoid* hitting the ball straight. I tried to cut a 2-iron shot off the tee, because I thought that any wood club would be a gamble.

The 18th hole at Medinah is a par 4 with a slight dogleg to the right, and I didn't want to drive through that dogleg and into the trees. So, I took a 2-iron and figured I would hit it with just enough cut to spin the ball gently from left to right and put it in the middle of the fairway.

I hit the ball straight, and at this particular stage of the game, I was hitting my 2-iron probably as far as I normally hit a 3-wood. I came over it and the ball went slightly left and into the trees.

I have had a lot of people ask me how I felt when I went looking for the ball in the trees. Did I figure I had blown the Open? Was I scared that I wouldn't have a shot? Was I prepared to waste a stroke just to get the ball back into the fairway?

All these questions are the very same ones that any player must answer as he heads into the trees with all the money riding on the last hole during a weekend match at the club. If you can keep a few rules in mind under such circumstances, I think you will develop into a much more successful trouble-shooter.

There is nothing, by the way, that is more unsettling to an opponent than to pull off a trouble shot at a critical moment. It is particularly effective if your opponent is out in the middle of the fairway licking his chops and waiting to hear your golf ball caroming off a tree or two.

The first thing I think you must consider under such circumstances is whether the risk of playing toward the green is worth the gamble. Next, you must wonder if it would be smarter to play the ball laterally, perhaps even away from the green, and hope for success on the next shot.

Figure, too, just how much of a gamble is involved. What is to be the reward if the gamble turns out well? Will the ball be on the green, or do you still have a chip shot or maybe a 75-yard approach shot remaining?

If you decide your only shot is away from the green, you must be prepared to lose a stroke—but possibly hit a good one on the next shot and save it. The main reason for playing laterally, or away from the green, is to avoid losing two strokes.

Frankly, I believe the worst thing you can do under such pressure and circumstances is to come up with some sort of compromise shot, something in between the two alternatives. Make your decision on what type of shot you want to play, and then try to hit it the way you plan it. Never play a half-gamble, a half-safe shot. This sort of compromise will ruin your score.

I have another word of advice on trouble shots, and that is to avoid playing for a miracle. Just keep in mind there are very, very few miracle shots accomplished in any round of golf; and for the most part, an attempted miracle shot may lead to a double-bogey—or worse. You realize, I hope, how damaging the double-bogey is to anybody's score.

I have known players who went for a miracle shot that called for the ball to travel low for the first 20 yards, go high for the next 15½ yards, low again for 23, and after clearing 100 yards of water, roll up a bank and across a bunker before getting to the putting surface.

This sort of foolishness—exaggerated though it is—is what I mean when I say *avoid the miracle attempt.* Even trying to hit a 6-iron shot through a break in the trees 40 yards in the air isn't the best choice in trouble situations.

Certainly there are times when you have to go for the miracle, but that is absolutely the last resort. I remember a while back in New Orleans, I had to hit one of those shots out of trees with a 6-iron. I had to hit it because any other type of safe shot would leave me with a 4-wood to the green. I was trying to win, and I took the big chance. I hit a tree, and I made double bogey. Miracles just don't happen—not very often, anyway.

I hate to say this, but my shot from the trees at Medinah wasn't all that tough. I had to keep the ball low for a few yards, 25 at the most, but there was plenty of room for me to get into the open once I got the ball under the limbs. My other choice was to play safe and chip back onto the fairway with Mahaffey.

But if he makes a par, and I get a 6, then we are all even again. My record for making par from the middle of the 18th fairway at Medinah wasn't too hot. In three of the previous four rounds, I had had the ball in per-

fect position off the tee, right out where Mahaffey was standing, and I made five every time. So, I figured if I chipped out and took four more strokes from the middle of the fairway, that would be a six and we'd be in sudden death.

In order to win, you must be willing to gamble at times, but not play foolishly.

My choice turned out to be pretty easy. I had to try to hit a low shot under the trees, and I had a good chance to make it work. I had a good lie. The ball was in grass in the rough, but it was "down-grain" because of the way the crowds had been tracking toward the green. My chief concern—really, my only concern—was to hit a low shot and not let it slip too far left.

I picked the 4-iron because from the middle of the fairway that is the club I would have used on a normal, 180-yard shot to the green. The distance wasn't a big problem, although I didn't want to hit too much club because there was a sand trap at the right of the green, right in my intended line of flight. Earlier in the week, I had made a bogey from the trap.

I turned the toe of the club down to decrease the loft. To get the shot under the limbs, I also moved my hands well in front of the ball and played the ball off my right foot. My plan was to hit the ball low and to the right, short of the bunker. The rest was routine.

I maintained super concentration, feeling I had planned the shot perfectly. I was confident I could hit the ball the way I wanted to, and I concentrated on keeping my tempo and not rushing the backswing. I also wanted to be sure to complete my backswing.

I did all this, and it worked. The ball stopped 10 feet from the putting surface and 60 feet from the pin. My chip shot was seven feet from the cup and when Mahaffey failed to sink his putt from 22 feet, I had two putts to win. I made the putt for par and the title.

My trouble shot worked.

11
The Warm-Up

For the remainder of the book I would like to take you on a playing lesson. I want you to come along with me as I replay my last 18 holes of the 1977 U.S. Open at Southern Hills Country Club in Tulsa, Oklahoma.

I will reconstruct each of the 68 shots; and the ideas and tips we have talked about in previous pages actually will come into practice on the fine, if somewhat warm, June morning.

I hit some good shots and some bad ones as I attempted to overtake Hubert Green. At the end, Hubert won by a stroke, 278 to 279.

There were times when I made some of the same mistakes I feel sure you make every now and then when playing your regular weekend game. I will explain why I made the bad shot—or the good one—and I will tell you how I went about implementing the stroke-saving tips we have discussed in earlier chapters.

Let's begin by going to the practice tee for 15 or 20 minutes of warm-up. I always like to start with the smaller clubs and then move up through the bag, hitting shots with every other club, and finally finishing by hitting a half-dozen shots with the driver.

After the practice tee, the next stop is the putting green, where another five or ten minutes will put the finishing touches on our warm-up. On the practice putting green, I never get overly excited or too discouraged if my putting is super or not-so-hot. I am working to get my putting rhythm going, nothing else.

Of course, if I have been working on a new grip or new putting stance, then I concentrate on the change in addition to setting my putting tempo for the day.

My starting time at Tulsa was 1:37 P.M., and that meant it was going to be warm—in the 90s, as a matter of fact—although there

Graham estimates he works 30 minutes on the practice tee and putting green before a tourament round. He has a routine whereby he begins with wedges and then hits shots with every other club on up through his driver, the last practice before the sand trap and putting green. (Photo by Dan Loftin)

was a bit of a breeze. When I play in warm weather, there are three pieces of equipment that I consider absolutely necessary.

First, I think you should wear a cap. This keeps the glare down and helps in judging distances and reading greens. Then, I always want to keep a good, dry glove on my hand. I get a much firmer grip wearing a glove, and I want it to fit very snug, not squeezing tight, but snug. I take the glove off when I putt because I believe I judge the speed of the greens better and get a finer touch. However, I know many players who wear their gloves when putting, so you probably should try both ways and decide for yourself. The third piece of equipment I believe to be essential in hot weather is a towel. It helps me keep my hands and grips dry, and also is wonderful for wiping the sweat off my face and neck.

When playing in hot weather, I find it is a good idea to try to drink water as often as possible. Drink frequently, but not a great deal at once.

I hear the starter calling us to the first tee. Let's get it on!

Graham prefers to wear a cap when playing "because it definitely cuts down the glare for me and helps me in judging distances and reading greens." The 1975 U.S. Open champion also believes it's best for him to putt without a glove "because I can judge the speed of the greens better and have a finer touch when I putt barehanded." (Photo by Jimmy Holt)

12
The Front Nine
(A Lesson)

No. 1—Too much right hand.
No. 2—Don't be foolish.
No. 3—A weight shift.
No. 4—Hit the wind cheater.
No. 5—The three-shot hole.
No. 6—Calm down.
No. 7—Play it safe.
No. 8—The big pitch.
No. 9—Lag it.

NO. 1 (447 YARDS, PAR 4)

A Pulled Drive

On the first hole I pulled my drive to the left. All week long it had been necessary to hit a lot of hooks off the tees in order to keep the ball in the fairway. By Sunday, it seemed as though I had created a monster that I could not control. I had difficulty all day control-ling my hook, and it got me in some real trouble on No. 17, as you may know.

I wanted to get to the left side of No. 1 if at all possible, because it makes for such a better approach iron, and that is a big part of improving your score. If you consider where the next shot comes from, it helps you avoid future trouble. On the first shot, however, I let up a little at impact and didn't hit through firmly on the drive. The right hand immediately took control and forced the ball on a pull-hook course.

The drive carried into the trees at the left side of the fairway, but didn't hit anything very hard and continued to roll, leaving me a 150-yard shot, which had to be kept low and come out between a very narrow opening in the trees. About all I could really hope for was to roll it down somewhere short of the

Hole No. 1   447 Yards, Par 4

This is a slight dogleg to the left. The ideal drive from the elevated tee is to the left side of the fairway. The green opens away from a rather large bunker at the right front. The green slopes left, and there is a smaller bunker at the left rear.

Graham drove into the left trees, played a trouble shot to the right front of the green, and chipped eight feet past for a two-putt, bogey 5.

green and try to make a good chip and one-putt for a par.

Trouble Shot

I had to play a 4-iron from a fair lie in short grass. Nothing restricted my back-swing or follow-through, so I played the ball well back in my stance. That was to keep the ball low. I also narrowed my stance because I didn't have to hit a real strong shot. The ball came out just fine. It didn't hit anything and it rolled to a stop about five feet in front of the green and just off the edge of the bunker on the right side.

A Bogey Beginning

The pin was in the left front and the green sloped away. I looked at it a little while and took my stance without a club in my hands. This is a routine preliminary action when I want to try to visualize where the ball is go-ing to land and how it is going to roll.

Looking more closely I saw the cup was on a little knob, so I took a 9-iron, choked it down, and chipped the ball a little strong. It was a touchy chip, because if the ball got go-ing too fast, once it got to the pin it could run off down the left side of the green. The whole shot was about 30 feet, and I stopped the ball maybe eight feet past the pin and two-putted for a bogey.

My first putt was a little weak, and as might be expected, the ball tailed off to the left. I played the putt at the right lip of the

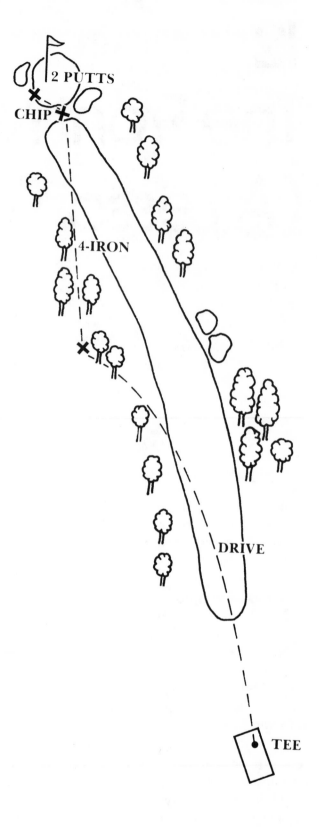

cup and just wanted to make a nice roll at the hole.

It really wasn't a very difficult putt, and if it had been on the fourth hole instead of the first, it would have been much easier. I think the first putt of a round is as difficult a putt as there is, and I would advise taking plenty of time on it. Remember, when you get back to the clubhouse after the round, that first putt counts just as much as the last putt.

NO. 2 (459 YARDS, PAR 4)

Another Pulled Drive

On the second hole a couple of significant developments occurred which I think are most important in any round of golf: (1) I got lucky on my drive; and (2) I kept my cool and avoided the double bogey which so often spoils a score.

For the second straight drive, I loafed just enough at impact to let my right hand control the shot too much, and I pulled the ball into the trees at the left of the fairway. The ball dropped down into the deep rough. This is where I considered myself lucky, for when the ball hit the tree, it could have dropped into the creek and cost me another stroke. It didn't.

Trouble Shot

I had absolutely no chance to reach the green on my second shot, so I began to plan

Hole No. 2   459 Yards, Par 4

This is perhaps the most demanding driving hole on the course. A drive must carry at least 220 yards over a creek and fairway bunkers. The premium spot off the tee is the right center of the fairway. The fairway generally slopes to the left toward the trees and trouble. The green is deep and narrow, falling toward both left and right, but without severe breaks.

Graham pulled his drive into the trees again; played a trouble shot back into the fairway, an approach iron onto the green, and two-putted for another bogey 5.

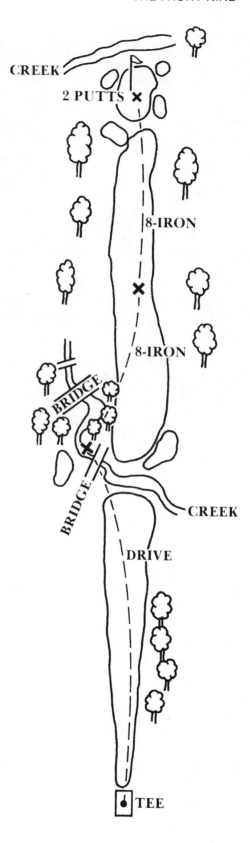

When hitting recovery shots from deep grass, or other trouble, it is always good to consider the next shot, too. In other words, don't try something foolish that might lead to more and deeper trouble. Pick out a target in the fairway and shoot for it. Don't just swing and hope you get the ball back into position for the next shot. (Photos by Jimmy Holt)

for a bogey. In other words, I wasn't going to try something foolish that might lead me into deeper trouble and more shots.

I elected to take an 8-iron and just punch it back out into the fairway. On a shot such as this, it is always good to consider the next shot too. From my position in the deep grass and trees, I really couldn't hope to advance the ball more than 50 yards. However, I made sure to watch for a good line and picked a target spot in the fairway. This is always a good idea when attempting trouble or recovery shots. Pick out a target. Don't just start swinging. On this particular shot, the fairway area wasn't too wide, so I conceivably could have punched the shot out of trouble on one side of the fairway and into trouble on the other. I have seen this happen.

The Mental Game

After I hit back to the fairway, I had to use the 8-iron once again, for now I was in the middle of the fairway 145 yards from the cup. So far, my planning had been solid, at least since the poor drive. From over in the trees I had figured if I could advance the ball 50 yards, I would be in good position with the possibility of still making a par. But above all, I would be standing there in the middle of the fairway with an 8-iron shot to the green. I felt reasonably sure I could make a bogey 5.

Still, as I walked along out of the rough and headed for the ball in the fairway, I thought to myself, "Gosh, it looks like you're gonna blow yourself right out of the tournament. You're gonna make two big bogies on the first two holes."

About that time, though, it dawned on me that the weather conditions were becoming a factor. It was hot and the wind was up. Scores might not be as good as I had figured when I started. At that time, I had told Norm [Graham's caddy is Norm Allerup] it probably would take three or four under par for us to win. On the way back to the fairway on this hole, I began to realize the course was playing very difficult, even if I had been driving the ball well.

Now I felt a score of one under, maybe even par, would win—and that's what happened. When playing conditions are difficult, you must realize that scores are going to be higher than normal. You must not become discouraged, especially early in a round. Although your score may not be as good as you had hoped, you must realize everybody else is likely to be having just as hard a time as you are—maybe even harder.

When the wind blows on a tough course with slick greens, which is the way most U.S. Open courses are, scores go up quickly. That's because it is very difficult to putt under such conditions, and it is also difficult to keep the ball in the fairway. That's the name of the game in golf—keep the ball in play and putt well.

I kept talking to myself as I walked out of the grass and trees. By the time I got to my ball in the fairway, I had convinced myself to keep shooting for the fairways and try to hit the greens in regulation. I figured every time I made a par, I was going to pass a lot more players than passed me. There aren't too many birdies made under such weather and pressure conditions. I just wanted to hang in there, because everybody was likely to have a tough time and there were plenty of holes ahead.

An Approach Iron and Two Putts

The third shot was 145 yards, and I didn't stay down on the shot. I hit it fair, a little thin. The ball wound up 30 feet to the right and short of the pin.

Now I had lost almost all hope of getting a "miracle" par. My goal on the 30-foot putt was to roll the ball close to the hole and hope it dropped in. If it didn't, I would take the bogey and consider myself lucky not to make double bogey 6. I two-putted for my second straight bogey 5.

NO. 3 (406 YARDS, PAR 4)

A Successful Correction

On the third tee we had to wait a couple of minutes while Rod Funseth and Jay Haas played their second shots. As most of us will do while standing with a golf club in our hands, I took a few practice swings, trying to find out just what was happening to cause me to pull-hook the driver on the first two holes.

I discovered that on my drive I felt like I was addressing the ball with my weight a little too far to the right side. I am sure I did this because I was trying to stabilize myself against the wind.

By keeping my weight on the right foot too long at impact, my hands were turning over as I hit the ball instead of turning over after I was well into my follow-through. This process of rolling the hands over is called pronation. I swung a couple more times and felt like my hands were turning over too fast on top of the ball. In other words, I was pronating too soon. The right hand was controlling everything and was causing the pull-hook drive.

When it came my turn to drive on the third tee, I made the first big adjustment of my round. As I addressed the ball, I moved my weight slightly more toward my left foot. Now I felt sure that when I made contact with the ball, my weight would have shifted well up onto the left side. This alteration would assure against a hook of any kind, and on this particular hole any little bit of a hook would ruin me. Here, you just can't play from the left rough. If I hooked again, I would have to chip out and play from there, and that would mean a third straight bogey.

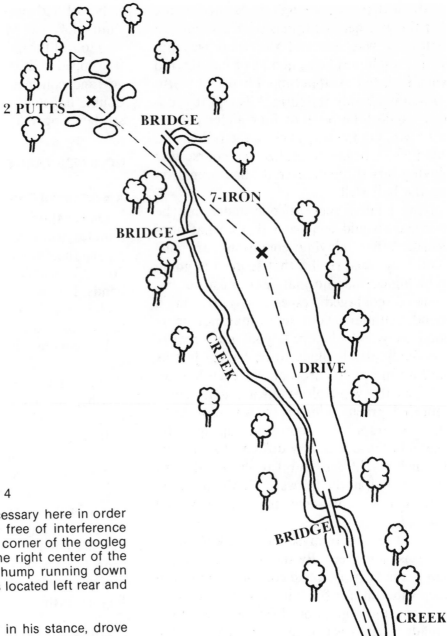

Hole No. 3   406 Yards, Par 4

Distance off the tee is necessary here in order for the second shot to be free of interference from the large trees at the corner of the dogleg left. The ideal drive is to the right center of the fairway. The green has a hump running down the center and the pin was located left rear and down a slope.

Graham, correcting a flaw in his stance, drove well, hit a 7-iron second shot, and two-putted for his first par.

The wind was blowing right to left, so whatever I did, the ball had to hold against this wind. With my weight well up toward the left side and my knees driving forward—in order to block out any possibility of a hook—I hit a dandy drive.

At my address, I picked out a cedar tree located on the right edge of the dogleg crook as my target. The ball stayed right on line, holding against the wind and moving ever so slightly to the left. It stopped rolling just a little to the right of center fairway. I was 150 yards from the pin.

In retrospect, this was an unusually important drive for me. For one thing, I had finally put the ball in position to hit a green in regula-

Moving the weight at address slightly toward the left foot helps shift the weight to the left side upon contact with the ball. This adjustment often works to assure against a hook, when the right hand controls everything and keeps the weight on the right foot too long at impact. (Photo by Jimmy Holt)

tion. Beyond that, I had been able to correct my pull-hook so quickly and so effectively that I could look to the driving holes with renewed confidence.

First Par of the Day

The pin was located on the left back and down a slope in the green. I wanted to put the ball on the green and get myself started, so I selected a 7-iron and hit the shot to within 25 feet of the cup.

The approach putt was very slick and had a big break to the left. I visualized the putt really breaking just before the hole, so I played well to the right of the cup. I rolled the putt well but it still got to the left of the hole, stopping about 12 inches past the cup. I tapped it in for my first par of the day.

NO. 4 (366 YARDS, PAR 4)

Driving into the Wind

Here the wind was blowing straight into my face, so I had to remind myself not to get all tightened up and let my weight get back too far to the right in an effort to brace, or stabilize, against the wind.

I used the same technique I had used on the third hole, moving my weight up toward the left. I aimed left center of the fairway and concentrated on hitting the ball low, under the wind, so to speak.

When I play a low shot into the wind, I tee the ball at approximately the same height as usual, but I concentrate on hitting just the top half of the ball. In other words, I just "pick" the ball off the tee. If you get out and practice this a little, you will know what I mean, and believe me it is really a stroke-saver on drives into the wind. If you work on it, you'll find that when you hit the ball properly it comes off the tee on a line drive and really bores into the wind. It isn't as difficult to hit as it might seem. A little practice will do the trick.

Birdie!

The key to this hole is the second shot because of two things: (1) If you hit the ball well off the tee, you are going to get an uphill lie;

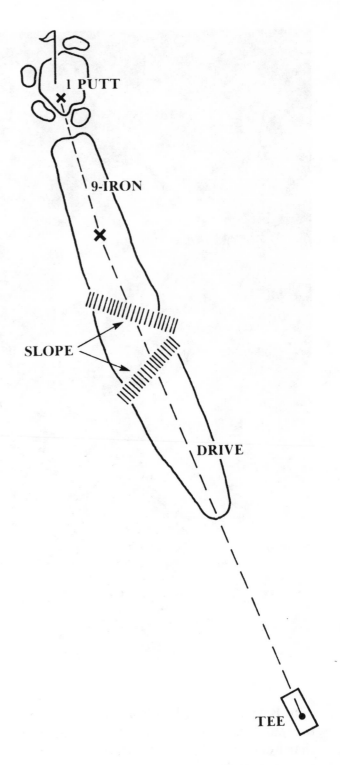

Hole No. 4 366 Yards, Par 4

From the tee, the flag flying in front of the clubhouse is visible. A drive played on a line just to the right of this flag is a good position from which to hit the approach iron up the hill to a two-level green which slopes both right and left as well as to the front. The fairway slopes sharply to the right, and the line just right of the clubhouse flag usually gives the golfer the proper bounce that sets up the approach shot.

Graham drove to the left center of the fairway, hit a 9-iron shot four feet below the cup, and made his first birdie of the round.

When you have an uphill shot, you should make allowance in yardage. If you are slightly uphill add 10 yards to the distance. If you are facing a long uphill shot, add 20 yards. Uphill shots also should play the ball a little forward in your stance. There is a tendency to pull the ball, too, so make sure you move your weight into the shot and don't be lazy and stay back on the right foot. (Photo by Jimmy Holt)

and (2) This green slopes severely, and with a slick putting surface you don't want to hit too far and have a downhill putt.

I estimated I had 110 yards left to the pin, and it was uphill and into the wind. When you have an uphill shot, you should make allowances in yardage. I use the following for-mula: slightly uphill, add 10 yards; extremely uphill on a long shot, add 20 yards.

The wind also makes a difference in club selection. It depends on the velocity, of course, but just a very slight breeze will mean 10 yards difference. These distances work the other way too. With the wind back of you, deduct 10 yards or more.

Anyway, I estimated I had a 110-yard shot, slightly uphill and into the wind. I picked a 9-iron for the shot. Normally, I hit a 9-iron in the 130- to 140-yard range, but because of the allowances I felt I had the proper club for the shot.

I must have made the correct calcu-lations, because the ball landed on the green and stopped about four feet from the pin, leaving me a relatively easy putt. It was straight, but because of the wind and the uphill nature of the terrain, I hit the putt quite firmly. It went on a perfect line and I had my first bird-ie of the day.

NO. 5 (614 YARDS, PAR 5)

A 3-Wood off the Tee

With the wind blowing behind me at a pretty good clip, I knew I would have to hit a driver almost perfectly to stay in the fairway at the dogleg landing area. I decided to hit a 3-wood off the tee instead.

I didn't hit the shot very well, and that add-ed to the other difficulties. The wind was blowing left to right, and I wanted to hold the 3-wood shot against the wind. I aimed left, at the edge of the trap on the left side of the fairway.

I tried to make sure I hit through the ball very hard in order to get the ball out to the dogleg, but I caught the ball a little high on the club face and this made it pop up. It went into the bunker where I was aiming. I was trying so hard to hit the ball hard that I messed up my timing. The result was the high hit, and when I didn't catch the 3-wood square, it was short and in the bunker. This same sort of error occurs frequently in pro-amateurs. An amateur tries to hit hard, gets his tempo

Hole No. 5   614 Yards, Par 5

This is the longest, and one of the more difficult, holes on the course. The landing area for the drive is narrow. There are trees all along both sides of the fairway and the green is well-trapped. A creek runs to the right side of the green down a sharp embankment. A hump runs across the green and makes reading putts quite difficult.

Graham used a 3-wood off the tee, and drove the ball into the left fairway bunker. He came out of the sand with a 6-iron, used the club again and went into a greenside trap. His blast was short. He two-putted for a bogey 6. It was to be his last bogey of the day.

off, and winds up losing distance, sometimes even digging into the ground back of the ball.

Getting Out of the Bunker

When you drive the ball into a fairway bunker on a par 5, the first thing you must understand is that you cannot get the ball on the green on your next shot. At least, you can't get on in two on most par-5 holes I've played. So, I heartily recommend that you keep your hands off fairway woods when you find yourself in such a situation. The extra 50 or 60 yards you may get by hitting a fairway wood from a bunker isn't worth the risk. It is a very, very difficult shot.

The important thing to remember is to make sure you get the ball out of the bunker.

Get it in position to put your third shot on, or very near, the green. When you are preparing to play a trouble shot, remember to plan ahead: "If I hit the ball perfectly, will it be on the green, or is it just going to be in front of the green? What happens if I don't hit it as I plan? Where will it go? Am I going to leave it here in the bunker? Am I going to knock it into the rough? What else could happen?"

I always try to impress upon my amateur partners that it usually takes them three shots to get on a par-5 hole. So go ahead and take a club which you know you can use to knock the ball out of the trap and back into the fairway. It really doesn't matter if your third shot is a little longer than you hoped. The big thing is to get it out of the bunker and back into play in the fairway.

In the bunker at the dogleg, I had a high lip about three feet in front of me. I had a good lie in the sand and the wind was blowing at my back. I felt like I could hit the ball about 175 yards, so I selected a 6-iron for the shot. The sand was just a little soft, but there was no problem with the lie and stance. I dug my feet in for a good, firm stance and swung about normal. The ball came out just fine. The long sand shot is a very difficult one to put on the green, but this sort of shot was really very easy. I just played it as though I was hitting from out in the fairway.

Another Trap

The wind was blowing left to right somewhere between 20 and 25 miles an hour, and from the middle of the fairway I figured I had a 6-iron shot remaining. The pin was tucked in back of a bunker on the extreme right edge of the green. To the right of the green, down a sharp bank, there is a creek. My first goal was to make certain I didn't let the ball get too far right and bounce down that bank. This was the main thing I wanted to avoid, for all I was trying to do was get out with a par.

I knew I was struggling. After a poor start,

I felt very good with my par on the 3rd and the birdie on the 4th. But now I needed to play this 6-iron shot well, or I could lose more ground. A poor shot to the right could really be trouble for me.

As a result, I played the 6-iron shot to the left, trying to hold the ball against the wind. I took a normal stance and turned a little so I was aiming just left of the green, figuring the wind to bring the ball back to the right a bit. I didn't hit the shot well, and pulled the ball into the left sand trap. The ball plugged deep down into the sand, and I faced a very, very difficult situation.

Looking at the 6-iron shot again, I realized—as so often happens—that I was trying to be absolutely sure I wouldn't let the ball get to the right. So I hit it a little too strongly and my hands turned over about like they did on the first two drives of the round.

My Last Bogey of the Day

Frankly, I much preferred going left into the trap than letting the ball go right and down that bank into the creek. Along about this time during the round it was a matter of the lesser of two evils. I was trying to hit the green, but I wound up with a somewhat difficult shot. I was standing in the trap with a very strong wind at my back and the green sloping away from me toward a creek.

I hit down into the sand, trying my old trick of knocking a divot of sand onto the green. The ball popped out onto the green. It rolled, as I had anticipated, but stopped about 12 feet from the cup. The putt broke from left to right and there was about a six-inch break. I gave the ball a nudge with the putter and it slipped along that slick green and eased about six inches past the cup, rolling right over the top edge of the hole.

It was a bogey 6, and as things turned out, it was my last bogey of the round. However, I was upset and concerned that I had had to struggle so hard to make a bogey on a par-5 hole. But again, I had a little talk with myself, saying that I couldn't allow the rather shaky start to upset me.

That's one of the important things to remember in playing a round of golf. You must realize that you have a lot of holes ahead, and each one of them is important. Try to play every shot as if it is the most important shot in the world, but convince yourself there is plenty of time to recover from the early bogies.

This sort of thinking does a couple of things for you. First, it helps you rebuild confidence for some of the shots ahead. More important, it keeps you concentrating so you don't lose interest and give up on the round.

NO. 6 (175 YARDS, PAR 3)

A Much-Needed Par

Along about now, what I really needed to accomplish was to get myself an old-fashioned, routine par. So at the tee, with the wind at my back, my plan was to hit the ball on the green and settle down a bit.

The wind was blowing pretty hard now, and I figured the shot was 175 yards downhill. I selected a 7-iron, and my plan was to get the ball up quickly and let it ride with the wind. In order to make certain I got the ball up fast and high, I played the ball a little farther forward in my stance. This enables you to hit a higher shot.

There was no problem with distance. Many times, with the wind at your back, you want to take advantage of the condition to hit

the ball farther. On this 7-iron shot, my goal was to get it high so the ball would come down straighter and stop sooner when it hit the green.

Actually, I was concentrating on staying a little bit behind the shot as I hit into it. In other words, I wanted to make sure I didn't move in front of the ball too quickly and have it come out on a line drive.

I needed to hit a good shot and I did. I put the ball on the green about 20 feet from the cup. It was a relatively straight-in putt and just slightly uphill. I gave the ball a good roll and it stopped for an easy tap-in and my par 3.

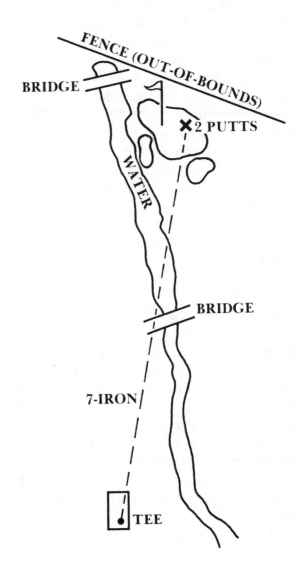

Hole No. 6   175 Yards, Par 3

Club selection is very important on this short par 3. The big trouble spots are the water at the left of the green and the out-of-bounds fence at the rear. Shifting winds add to the club selection difficulty.

Graham hit a 7-iron, allowing the shot to ride with a strong wind. The ball stopped 20 feet to the right of the flag. He two-putted for a par 3.

Time for a Change

As I was walking off the green, I resorted to one of my favorite superstitions. I changed golf balls.

I had been struggling for six holes, and I needed a change. I have this little superstition, just like most athletes. It really doesn't mean a thing, except it is something I can do that makes me feel like it will get things going for me again.

Not only did I change golf balls, but I got one with a different number. I had been using a No. 3, and I changed to a No. 6. I played with this ball for the rest of the way. I don't have a number preference, any that works is okay with me. On this particular round, it was No. 6.

I frequently am asked how long you should use a golf ball. Normally, I play with the same ball for five or six holes. I don't change the ball unless something bad has happened—like a double bogey, for instance. Of course, if I scuff it or bruise it, I'll make a change. Otherwise I use perhaps three balls a round. I really don't see any need to set a specific number of holes for a ball. As the old saying goes, "Ride a good horse till he falls."

Naturally, most amateurs can't change golf balls as frequently as a professional. Golf balls are expensive, and there is no doubt in my mind that a golf ball will do a good job for you for 18 holes. Just look at Al Geiberger. He only used one golf ball that day in Memphis when he shot 59!

When I was an amateur and golf balls were a little harder to come by, I played more than 18 holes with one ball many, many times.

Lots of times, though, you will scuff or cut a ball or knock it out of bounds. You are better off if you have a new ball under such circumstances.

For the moment, I had achieved my goal by getting the par. I had needed to get myself calmed down a little, get my game working again, and most of all get my confidence back. I had succeeded.

In looking back on the day, this little par-3 hole was of tremendous importance to me.

NO. 7 (383 YARDS, PAR 4)

A Safe Tee Shot

This hole is a dogleg left that goes up the hill. The wind was blowing from right to left, and I used a 3-wood off the tee to make sure I didn't get the ball too far down the fairway and onto a slope that takes everything into the right rough.

My stance for the 3-wood drive was pretty square, and I decided to use the wind on the shot. I aimed the ball up the right side of the fairway. With this right edge as my target, and the wind blowing hard from right to left, I wanted the wind to work at drawing the ball into the fairway. It did just that. I hit the 3-wood shot very full, and the ball wound up just a little to the right of center in the fairway.

Caution Dictates My Second Shot

When I got up to the ball, I found the pin was tucked into the extreme right front edge of the green. It was just over the trap and near a creek on the right side, a tough pin placement.

At the same time, I found that the trees which sat along the edge of the right rough hung out across the fairway. From my position in the fairway, a shot toward the flag would have to carry over the trees. The wind continued to be brisk, and I figured it would take an 8-iron, possibly a 7-iron, to go up over the limbs and reach the flag. It was decision-time again.

I decided at this point it might be better for me to try a low shot, a shot that would take me around the limbs and onto the green. I knew it would mean I would have a longer putt, 25 feet or so, but with that pin sitting on that narrow neck, and the wind blowing, the shot over the trees was quite risky.

If I hit the ball high enough to get it over the trees, thereby letting the wind take over, I

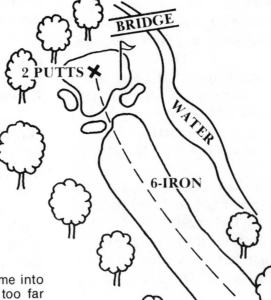

Hole No 7   383 Yards, Par 4

The trees at the right of the fairway come into play if the golfer lets his tee shot get too far right. The green is almost 100 feet wide, and a difficult pin placement is to the extreme right.

Graham's 3-wood tee shot went to the right center of the fairway, and the trees determined he would attempt a cut 6-iron shot under the limbs. His shot stopped 25 feet to the left of the pin, and he two-putted for his par 4.

felt I would have absolutely no control of the shot. I could wind up with anything, any kind of score, and blow myself completely out of the tournament.

I was already two over par. If I took a big gamble now—and it didn't pay off—I would be out of contention no matter how well I might play in the holes to come. So I decided on the low, around-the-trees, out-of-the-wind shot and selected a 6-iron.

Taking my stance over the ball, I found the ball was a little bit below my feet. I played the ball back a little toward the right foot, because I wanted to cut the ball and make it hold against the wind and stay under the limbs. My hand position was routine, hands just slightly in front of the ball. As I hit into the shot I made sure I kept my head well up over the ball. In other words, I wasn't really in behind the shot very much. When I moved through the shot, I tried to cut it just a little. I wasn't trying to put a big cut on it; I was just

The downhill lie shot will see the ball slide a little to the right, so aim left. Also play the ball back a little bit in the stance. Make sure you hit down through the shot with the club following the slope of the hill. Above all, never try to lift the ball with the club. (Photo by Jimmy Holt)

routine. There was very little break, and I rolled a good approach putt down and made my par.

A Lesson for You

Again, I feel that this was an important hole for me. I had parred the 6th and got a good steady par on this one, although I had managed it from somewhat adverse conditions, having to play the second shot around, rather than over, the trees. The par built a little more confidence for me, at what I now recognize as a very critical time in the round.

This hole demonstrates my theory that you play each shot as it comes. I had kept myself out of any severe trouble by hitting a 3-wood off the tee. The second shot was not in super position, but I had a choice. When I made the decision, I worked on the shot without any other distractions. In other words, I put the alternative shots out of my mind and tried to hit the shot at hand as best I could.

I wanted to make a safe shot, and I did. The putt was more a test of speed than anything, and I had it rolling well enough for a tap-in par.

This is the sort of planning—involvement, if you will—that you should adopt in achieving lower scores. Had I played over the trees toward the pin, I might have hit the ball well and made a birdie. But anything short of a super shot easily could have resulted in a bogey—or worse.

When planning your strategy under such conditions, I again want to emphasize how important it is to weigh every factor you can imagine. At this point in the round, a double bogey, for instance, would have finished my chances.

It was an important par for me.

NO. 8 (215 YARDS, PAR 3)

Stopped by the Wind

This is a long, hard par 3. The first day I had hit a 4-wood right up on the green. On the second day the pin had been tucked in the

playing a relatively safe shot onto the green in order to putt. I was not trying to get the ball close to the hole, for I had already decided against that sort of gamble. When you make such a decision, do not try to change something in the course of your swing. Make your decision and then follow that plan. Any sort of alteration can mean trouble.

The ball stopped about 25 feet from the pin. It was not a difficult putt; it was rather

Hole No. 8   215 Yards, Par 3

This is a long, difficult par 3, made even harder by a stout breeze coming against the golfers. A creek at left rear and strategically placed bunkers add to the difficulty. The front half of the green slopes forward and to the left. A hump extends through the center, so the back part of the green slopes away.

Graham used a 4-wood into the wind, and his tee shot came to rest 15 yards short of the green. He pitched a sand wedge shot over the bunker and down the slope to within three feet of the pin. He one-putted for a par 3.

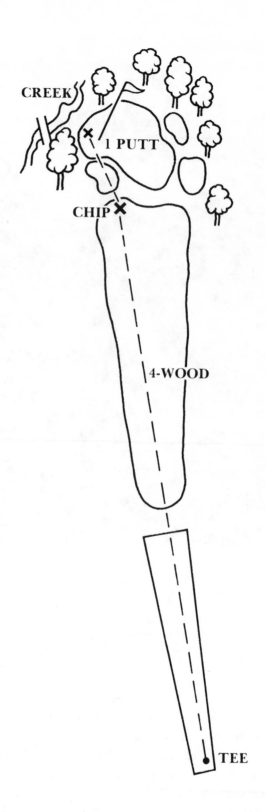

left back corner, so I had hit a 3-wood. It was too much club and the ball had gone over the green and into the lake at the left rear of the green. On the third round I had put the ball smack in the center of the green with a 4-wood.

On this final round the wind was blowing hard, and they had the pin back on the left again, just over a trap. I wasn't sure I could reach the flag with a 4-wood, but I felt I would reach the center of the green. More important, I knew I could not knock a 4-wood shot over the green as I had done with the 3-wood.

I didn't really try to hit the 4-wood exceptionally hard, because I felt I had plenty of club. The wind, though, was blowing harder than I thought. I placed the ball on the tee at normal height. By the way, I always set the ball up on a tee if I have a chance. By that I mean that even if I'm on a par-3 hole, I use a wooden tee. I figure I can control the clubface action on the ball much more accurately this way, so I never just toss the ball down on the grass and hit it from there, as you sometimes see other players do.

The 4-wood was hit well, probably as well as I can hit the club, but the wind gusted and my ball dropped down about 15 yards short of the putting surface. The 4-wood shot had traveled far less than my normal 215-230-yard range. I estimated it went maybe 180 yards—and believe me, I had hit it well.

Perfect Pitch

Now I was faced with a little pitch shot over a sand trap. I was fortunate to have a good lie so I could use my sand iron, because this was a very difficult little shot. The green was running slightly downhill to the flag, and I picked as my target area a three-foot square of fringe just over the trap. In order to get the ball close, I knew I had to have the ball land on the fringe, or just on the edge of the putting surface. I did not, above all, want to mess with the trap.

I took the sand iron and opened the club face quite a bit. I choked down on the shaft in order to take a shorter swing than usual, but still hit it with a nice crisp stroke. By moving my hands down the shaft of the club—choking it, so to speak—I could hit hard and crisply and not worry about being lazy on this shot. This also meant I could get a little more spin on the ball. This was most important, because the green was running downhill, away from me.

To make this shot work, I had to hit the target area. The fringe was short, so I really wasn't too worried about what would happen if the shot landed on the fringe and not the putting surface. As it turned out, the ball carried over the trap by about five feet and landed just on the edge of the green. It took a good bite, an exceptionally good bite, after a couple of bounces, and wound up about three feet from the hole.

This was as good a pitch shot as I had hit in the entire tournament. It worked because I was able to open the club face, choke down on the shaft, and hit down and through the shot firmly, even though I had a total of 20 yards to work with, maybe less.

Pitching Tips

I really didn't have much choice of the type of shot to try over the bunker. Clearing the trap, of course, was my first goal. Sometimes, if the grass is short and the ball is clos-er to the green than this one, I will use a chip shot. This is where I will hit a 7-, 8-, or 9-iron and hit the ball lower landing on the fringe or edge of the green with little or no backspin. This can be a very effective shot and is easily perfected by practice. However, when I am 10 or 15 yards away, as I was here on the 8th hole, I always use the sand iron or pitching wedge. It must be hit crisply and played to take the spin and stop. A few practice sessions will allow you to get the feel of both the chip and pitch shots. You will discover just about what to expect in the way of the ball rolling after it hits the ground.

These little chip and/or pitch shots are super stroke-savers, and they are worth every minute you can spare practicing them. The chip shot is used right around the edges of the greens, when you try to get the ball onto the putting surface as quickly as possible. You want to get the ball rolling very soon, so you hit it quite low. You put very little spin on the ball, and hit with no loft, or as little as possible. The most effective chip shot is the one that stays close to the ground, then skips and starts rolling immediately after landing.

The pitch, such as the one I have described on the 8th hole, is hit farther onto the green if there is working room. This shot, with the pitching wedge or sand iron, goes higher and has backspin when it strikes the green.

The pitch-and-run is a combination of both the chip and pitch, and it really is not a hard shot to learn. It is nothing more than a lofted chip shot. It is very useful, and probably may be perfected more easily than any of the stroke-savers around the greens. The main thing is to practice hitting the ball crisply, for this is the key to the shot. Concentrate on hitting the ball solidly. You simply cannot become proficient with the pitch-and-run if you are lazy hitting the shot. You must hit it firmly and learn that feel of control. With practice, you will learn how to judge your distance and the speed of the shot.

The pitch, or pitch-and-run, is used over

traps where the fringes are fluffy or the green is grainy. You are much better off to go ahead and hit farther onto the green with more loft and spin on a grainy putting surface. Also, I recommend the more lofted shot if you are going uphill. Attempting to judge the speed and distance of a chip shot on a grainy green is tedious business. You are far better off to hit a pitch shot closer to the hole, for you then have less distance to worry about the ball rolling on a grainy surface. In such a situation it's the grain, not you, that controls the direction and speed of the ball's roll.

All these little stroke-savers are vital to scoring, and again, I want to remind you that these shots—just like the driver or any others—require a target. Nothing good will happen when you simply take the sand iron or wedge and flop the ball up in the general direction of the cup.

The same is true of the chip shot. When playing this little low-running chip shot, I pick out a spot on the edge of the green where I want the ball to land and start running without any spin. This is where your practice pays off, for with a little work you will know how far the ball is going to roll.

As is the case most of the time, the lie of the ball makes a big difference in the type of shot you attempt. On this particular pitch shot, I had a good lie. The ball was sitting up nicely in the grass, not down firmly on the ground, and this lie allowed me to use the sand iron. This club was absolutely necessary for me at the time, because there was no way I could get enough spin on the ball to stop it after going over the trap, landing on the fringe—or edge of the green—and rolling downhill toward the pin. A pitching wedge or 9-iron just doesn't offer enough loft or spin possibilities for this type of shot.

I mentioned that you must have a target area for any shot. I should tell you now that you also must have a target on the ball itself.

When I hit a pitch shot, I place the club back of the ball. There is a little space, a crack if you will, between the club face and the ball. That's where I am aiming and looking when I hit the shot. I try to slip the club under the ball, right in that tiny fraction of an inch back of the ball. Slipping the club right underneath the ball lofts it and puts spin on it. If you look on top of the ball, you will hit your shot too low. It is just a matter of opening the club face and letting the club slide underneath. This really takes some practice and patience, because it is not an easy shot to learn. It is like putting, for you must "feel" the club into the ball.

NO. 9 (373 YARDS, PAR 4)

Driving Into the Wind

The drive here was into the wind, and I hit a good one, positioning the ball into the center of the fairway. My target off the tee was the edge of the left rough. I wanted to cut the ball just a little and let it slide to the right.

Because I was driving into the wind, I reminded myself not to get my weight too far on the right side in an effort to stabilize myself in the breeze. I wanted to make certain as I moved into the shot that I got my weight up onto the left side and drove hard with my legs. This would block any chance of the ball going to the left. Remember, I had not hit the driver since the fourth hole, and I had gone to the left twice in the first four driving holes.

On this shot, let your legs drive forward in to the shot. You actually are letting your weight get over to your left side good and strong. Your knees are driving in, with your right knee driving up toward your left and your left knee going on through toward the target.

All this weight shift to the left side occurs before the clubhead gets to the ball. As you swing in toward the ball, make sure you get the weight off the right foot. If you stay on the right foot just a little too long, it will allow the hands to roll over too quickly. If you make sure the weight is on the left side as you

Hole No. 9   373 Yards, Par 4

The target off the tee into a prevailing wind is just right of the center of the fairway. Uphill on the approach iron, the hole plays longer than listed. The green is two-level and slopes severely from the center to the front. The upper level slopes right.

Graham drove to the middle of the fairway, well past the bunker at the corner of the dogleg. Hitting uphill and into the wind, Graham used a 9-iron for his second shot. The ball was to the right and 15 feet beyond the pin. He nicked the cup on his approach putt and knocked in the short second putt for a par 4.

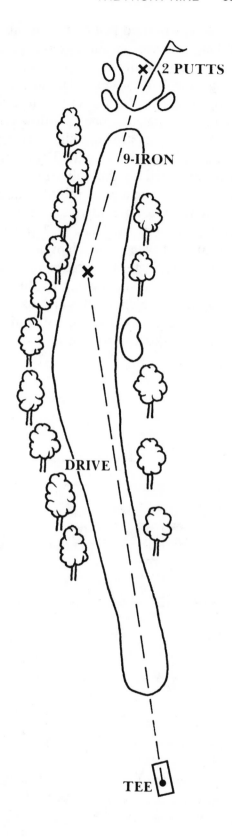

come in, and if the knees are going toward the target as you make contact, the clubhead will continue straight forward and will not allow you to "spin off" the ball.

You are guilty of "spinning off" a shot when you get to the ball and your left leg starts turning back away from the ball. Your right leg comes in and causes the hands to turn over on top of the shot. Or, the right leg coming in may cause you to lose control of your weight and hit a big push or slice. However, if you make sure that you get over on your left side good and strong, the club will not turn over. You then may make sure you put a cut on the shot.

This time everything went well, and I did, indeed, put a nice little cut on the ball as I drove it into the middle of the fairway. My second shot turned out to be quite similar to the one I had on the 4th hole where I had made my first birdie.

An Approach and a Lag

I had a 9-iron shot to the green. It was perhaps 110 or 115 yards uphill and slightly into the wind. I picked the 9-iron, as I had done on the 4th, because of the elevation and the wind. I put the approach shot just to the right and a little behind the hole, leaving a 15-foot putt. It was touchy, too, for it was downhill and really slick.

Now, I remind you of my rule about putts: When you are on slick greens and you get those "downhillers," all you want to do is "lag" the ball close enough so that it either drops in the cup or stops very close. I feel this is an *absolute rule*, one to follow every time.

When you are on slick greens, don't "charge" any kind of putt. Try to figure your putting speed so the ball stops close to the cup. Don't take a good roll at it, and remember that on fast greens you have to play more break on every putt. You probably should allow at least twice as much break as you do on normal-speed greens, because you have to figure where the ball is going to stop. That was really my problem on this approach, or "lag" putt. Where was it going to stop?

If you take a normal stroke—with normal speed—on slick greens, you are going to go by on the high side of the cup every time. That's because you are hitting the ball too hard for it to take the break. It is going to be slipping past the cup three or four feet.

After a while, these three- and four-footers will eat you alive. You miss one or two of them and then you are in real trouble. Your confidence sags, and this uneasiness begins to back up right on through your entire game. Finally, you are just trying to finish, trying to get into the clubhouse and not worrying about your score, which undoubtedly has gone up five or six strokes over normal.

I made a pretty good pass at the first putt. The ball caught the top of the cup and "lipped out," 10 or 12 inches. I tapped it in and made the turn two over par.

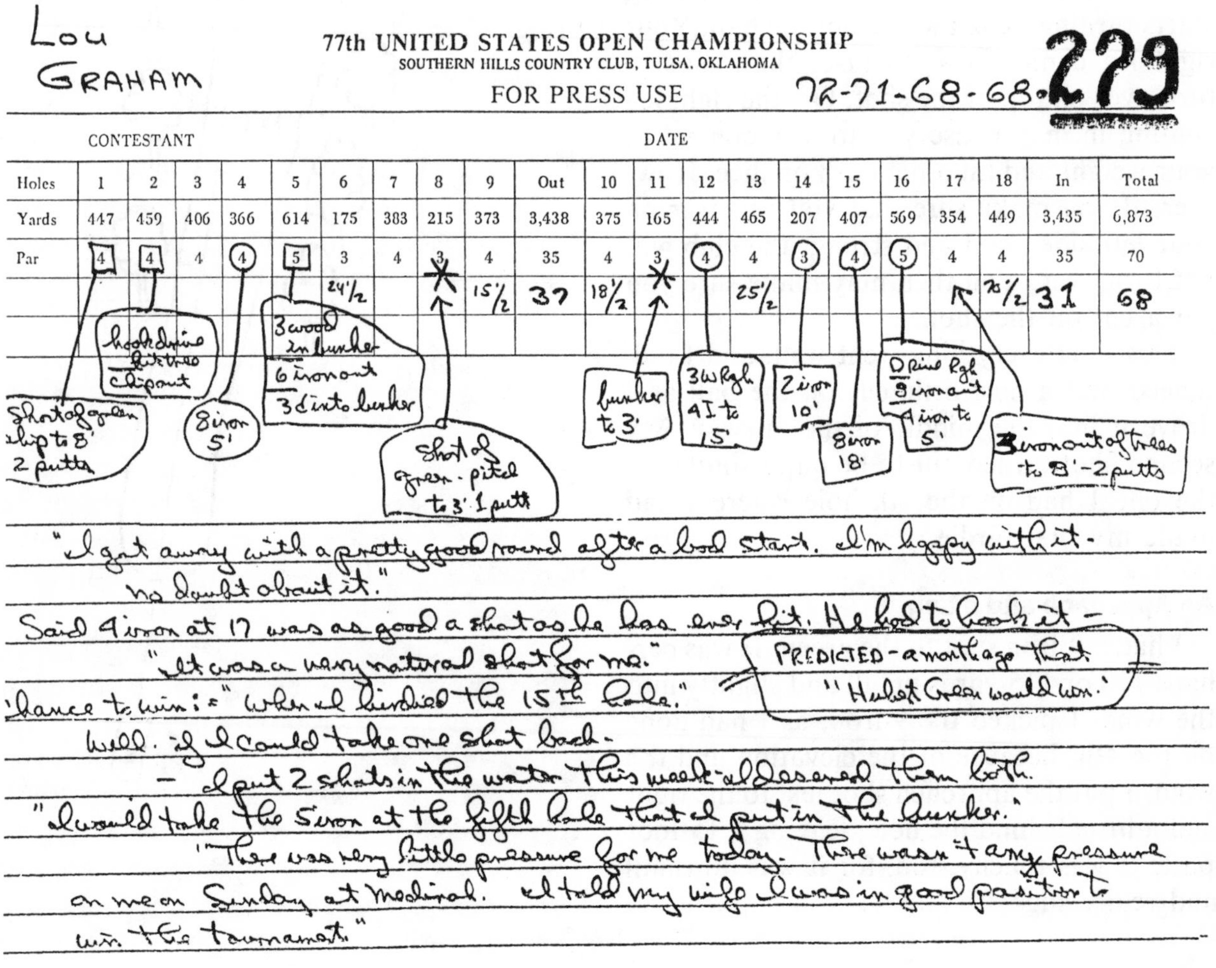

Lou Graham — 77th UNITED STATES OPEN CHAMPIONSHIP — SOUTHERN HILLS COUNTRY CLUB, TULSA, OKLAHOMA — FOR PRESS USE — 72-71-68-68 = 279

Holes	1	2	3	4	5	6	7	8	9	Out	10	11	12	13	14	15	16	17	18	In	Total
Yards	447	459	406	366	614	175	383	215	373	3,438	375	165	444	465	207	407	569	354	449	3,435	6,873
Par	4	4	4	4	5	3	4	3	4	35	4	3	4	4	3	4	5	4	4	35	70

Handwritten annotations on scorecard:

Hole 4/5 area: 24½; Hole 8: ✳ 15½; Out: 37; Hole 10: 18½; Hole 11: ✳; Hole 13: 25½; Hole 17: 20½ 31; In: 68

- Shot off green, chip to 8' 2 putts
- hook drive bunker chip out
- 8 iron 5'
- 3 wood in bunker / 6 iron out / 3rd into bunker
- Short of green - pitch to 3' 1 putt
- bunker to 3'
- 3W rough 4I to 15
- 2 iron 10'
- 8 iron 18'
- Drive rough 8 iron out / 4 iron to 5'
- 3 iron out of trees to 8' - 2 putts

"I got away with a pretty good round after a bad start. I'm happy with it. No doubt about it."

Said 4 iron at 17 was as good a shot as he has ever hit. He had to hook it—

"It was a very natural shot for me."

'chance to win:' "When I birdied the 15th hole."

Well - if I could take one shot back.

— I put 2 shots in the water this week - I deserved them both.

"I would take the 5 iron at the fifth hole that I put in the bunker."

"There was very little pressure for me today. There wasn't any pressure on me on Sunday at Medinah. I told my wife I was in good position to win the tournament."

PREDICTED - a month ago that "Hubert Green would win."

13
The Back Nine
(A Lesson)

NO. 10 (375 YARDS, PAR 4)

An Excellent Drive

The tee shot is the key to this hole, and for this round the wind wasn't the least bit helpful. The wind was blowing from right to left, and while this is a short dogleg right, you must drive the ball across the dogleg corner of the fairway. However, you do not want to knock it through the fairway into the left side because of the severe rough and trees.

I took a 4-wood and hit a cut shot again, just a little cut so as to hold the ball against the right-to-left breeze. It was one of the best 4-wood shots I hit all week. The ball stopped right in the middle of the fairway.

The driving situation called for a shot similar to the one on No. 9. I made certain I got my weight up on the left side as I made impact with the ball. This was to prevent any kind of hook. A hook would really mess you up here, because it would turn this hole into a bogey right away.

To get the cut-shot action required for the type of 4-wood I wanted to hit, I moved my left hand a little up on top of the shaft. This was so that when I hit into the ball, I would get a little fade out of the shot. I also took the club back a little bit straighter than normal, and on the downswing I made certain the left hand pulled through the shot good and hard. I swung with the left hand on top, holding the

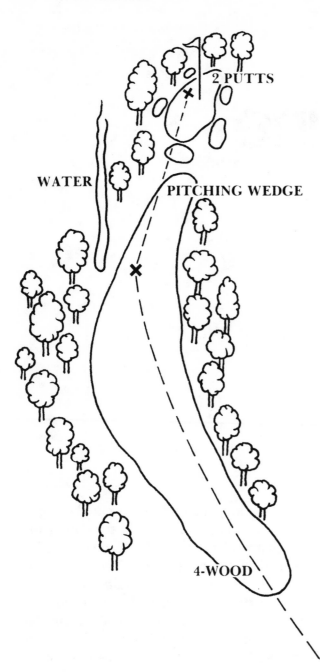

WATER

PITCHING WEDGE

2 PUTTS

4-WOOD

TEE

Hole No. 10   375 Yards, Par 4

The tee shot here must stay to the left of the trees at the right of the dogleg. A fairway wood or long iron is adequate off the tee. The second shot is quite short, but the green is elevated and pin placement difficult to determine.

Graham hit one of his best 4-wood shots off the tee, putting the ball across the dogleg with a slight cut and in the middle of the fairway. His wedge shot to the pin was 18 feet from the cup, and he two-putted for a par 4.

club so it would slide across the ball with a slightly open face. This cut-shot action would hold the ball to the right against the wind and keep it on a straight line of flight across the dogleg and into the fairway.

The shot came off exactly as I planned it, and now I was beginning to feel myself getting into the chase. I had parred four straight holes, hitting every shot just about the way I wanted to, and really only having the slightest bit of disappointment when I didn't reach the green on the tee shot at No. 8. (That's where my 4-wood was caught in the wind gust.)

Par Again

When I reached my ball in the fairway at the 10th, I had a fine lie and a shot of perhaps 105 yards. It was uphill to an elevated green and the wind was slightly against me. I calculated that I had a good, solid pitching wedge shot remaining. I hit the wedge shot 18 feet past and just to the right of the cup.

The putt was a downhiller again, breaking about one and one-half feet from left to right. It was really fast, and my plan was to just ease the ball down and make certain I left the putt close if it didn't drop.

I hit a good approach putt. As a matter of fact, I almost made this one, just as I had almost made the one at No. 9. But, I hit it a little too hard and the ball didn't break quite enough. It stayed on the high side of the cup until it got just even with the hole. Then it dropped down and left me a comeback putt of about 14 or 15 inches. I made it for a par 4.

My putts on the last two holes were beginning to add to my confidence, although I really could not conceive that I was very shortly to get involved in the thick of the fight against Hubert Green. The approach putts here and on the 9th green are things that turn a competitor on, for both were difficult putts, but both were hit well and kept me concentrating. I felt as though any minute now they'd start dropping.

NO. 11 (165 YARDS, PAR 3)

From Tee to Bunker

The wind seemed to be easing off a bit, but I committed a key error in my thinking on this hole. I let indecision creep into my mind while I was actually swinging the club into the shot.

This is a little hole, the shortest one on the course, and it is about 165 yards slightly downhill. The wind, or what there was of it, was coming from right to left. I decided to hit a 6-iron. Rather, I *almost* decided to hit a 6-iron.

After making the club selection, I went into the swing and for some reason I began to let myself believe I had a little too much club— since the hole was slightly downhill and there was little appreciable wind.

I felt myself begin to ease into the shot just

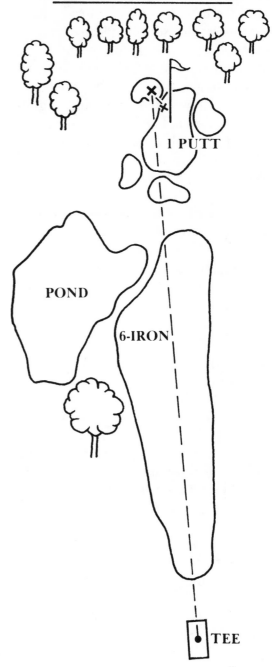

Hole No. 11   165 Yards, Par 3

This is the shortest hole on the course, but it is well trapped and the right-to-left wind seems to swirl, making club selection difficult at times. The green is narrow at the rear and wide in front.

Graham played a 6-iron for his tee shot pulled it slightly and wound up in the back bunker. He hit his 24-foot trap shot to within two feet of the cup. He made the putt for a par 3.

a little bit as I began to bring the club down toward the ball. As we have already discussed, when you let this sort of indecision creep into a shot, you are asking for trouble. I let my right hand start in too strongly, and when I began easing off with it, the left hand just quit. This allowed the right hand to grab full control of the shot. It came in so strong that it caused the club to turn over and created a pulling action to the left.

What I should have done, of course, was to use the 6-iron, but choke down on it a little and go ahead and hit through the shot more solidly. Instead, I committed the worst of errors: I let up on a shot.

The result was that the ball landed on the back left edge of the green and jumped into the bunker.

A Clutch Par

Now my emotions were churning. A couple of minutes earlier I was allowing myself—for the first time in several holes—to begin to think about a good score and a run at Hubert. So what happens? I was standing in a sand trap and facing the realization that another bogey would be too much that day.

I had begun to look at scoreboards around the course. I don't usually do this until late in the tournament, for I prefer to play my game and the course until it gets down to a one-on-one situation.

But standing there in the bunker, I knew that another bogey would put me too far back. For one thing, I was two over par for the day, three over for the tournament. Hubert, at last count, was four under par for the week. That meant I was seven strokes behind and Hubert was playing steady, last-round golf. I simply could not afford another bogey.

I had a good lie in the sand. It was an uphill lie and the texture of the sand was fairly firm. I felt that I had a good chance to get up and down in two strokes, because from my position in the bunker I thought I could get some spin on the ball.

The overall distance of the bunker shot was about 24 feet, which isn't too long. From my lie, I blasted the ball out in good shape. It landed five feet short of the hole, about where I had hoped it would land, and it rolled right up to the cup for a tap-in par.

Again, I had hit a shot as planned, and it came at a great time for me. I had set up on the sand shot with the ball forward just a little and the weight back on my right foot. With this stance, as I hit into the shot the club comes up quickly. I always try to hit three or four inches back of the ball, and since I had been hitting uphill on this shot, I had hit the ball harder than if I had been swinging from a flat lie or stance. This is because you swing along the contour of the sand. In other words, on an uphill stance you have to swing down and then up.

With a bit of practice, you can learn to judge the difference in the angle of the sand and how it will affect the ball coming out of the bunker. When you are on a downhill slope the ball comes out lower and runs more, so you don't hit the shot quite as hard.

NO. 12 (444 YARDS, PAR 4)

The "All-American" Golf Hole

I believe just about everybody who has ever played or seen Southern Hills Country Club picks this hole among the toughest on the course. I understand Ben Hogan rates it as the "All-American" golf hole.

I had used a 3-wood off the tee here on two of the three previous rounds. The one time I had hit my driver, I drove through the fairway on the right. The ball came to rest against a tree and I had to chip out for a bogey.

The hole doglegs around a sand trap, and with the wind coming a little behind us and left to right, I selected a 3-wood off the tee. After the dogleg, the hole goes down the hill toward the green. There is a creek that comes out on the left which forms a couple of little ponds across the front and along the right side of the green.

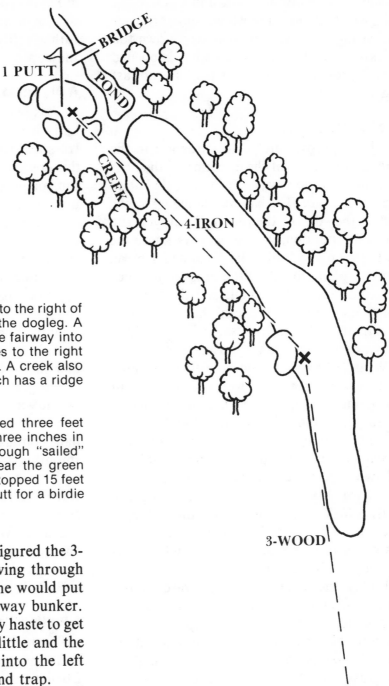

Hole No. 12 444 Yards, Par 4

The best driving target here is just to the right of the large bunker in the corner of the dogleg. A strong drive may carry through the fairway into trees at the right. The green slopes to the right toward a pond and is well trapped. A creek also guards the front of the green which has a ridge running through the center.

Graham's 3-wood tee shot stopped three feet right of the fairway bunker and three inches in the rough. His 4-iron from the rough "sailed" across the corner of the trees near the green and over the front lake. The ball stopped 15 feet from the flag, and he made the putt for a birdie 3.

It's a really testy hole, and I figured the 3-wood would keep me from driving through the fairway, yet at the same time would put me just to the right of that fairway bunker.

I hit the 3-wood fine, but in my haste to get on with the shot, I pulled it a little and the ball rolled about three inches into the left rough along the edge of the sand trap.

I think the reason I pulled my tee shot is because I accelerated too fast and cut my backswing short. In other words, I was so anxious to get to the ball, I didn't get the club all the way up to the top of the backswing. This error in tempo made me try to force the club back down in order to get the distance I felt I needed with the 3-wood.

With everything going too fast, my right

shoulder came out and over and I pulled the ball. Most of the time when you start your backswing too fast, you also start down too quickly from the top. That's what happened here. I probably tried to hit the ball too fast and too hard.

The "Sailer"

I had approximately 210 yards left to the flag, and because of the direction of the dogleg, the wind now was coming a little left to right in my face. The ball was sitting up nicely, just in the edge of the rough. When you run into this situation, you can always figure the ball is going to "sail." By "sailing" I mean you are going to get a little grass in between the club face and the ball, and the ball will come out squirting. It doesn't have any backspin on it, and usually a "sailer" will go 20 or 25 yards farther than a normal shot.

With 210 yards to the hole, I would normally use a 2-iron. However, because the ball was going to sail, I knew I had to subtract 20 or 25 yards and select a club that I usually could hit 180 to 185 yards. I selected a 4-iron. When you are going to hit a sailer, first back off two or three clubs and then go after the shot hard. If you ease into a sailer, it's going to fly a little, but it will slip off the club face one way or the other. Hit it hard, though, and it's going to come out pretty straight, without much hook or slice.

I play the sailer farther forward in my stance. That's so I can be sure to get the club under the ball and get it up in the air. Most of the time when you face a sailer situation, the ball is going to be sitting up high in the grass, and 50 or 60 percent of the time it is going to fly out regardless of how you hit it. In order to control it and get good distance, play the ball forward in your stance and hit it hard.

I hit with a 4-iron and the ball came out well for me. It sailed out of that rough and carried across the corner of the tall trees and over the front pond where it landed on the green maybe 25 or 30 feet short of the hole. It was high enough coming in that it bounced rather softly and stopped about 15 feet from the cup.

A Big Lift for Me

This was the big lift of the round for me. I had hit the ball close from a sailing lie over trees and water. Just to put a second shot on this green is a real boost, but to plan one from the rough and make it come off really gave my emotions and confidence a lift.

I knew that the 12th was going to be a hard hole for a lot of the people in back of me. With the pressures that were building now, it was going to be hard for some of the players to make a par, and here I sat with a real chance to birdie the hole. The sailer had me all "pumped up" and when I began to study my putt, I had that great feeling that comes now and then—I felt I was a cinch to sink it!

The putt broke slightly from left to right and it was a little uphill. I read the break as about three or four inches. I visualized the ball coming off the putter's face, rolling smoothly for 12 or 14 feet and then beginning to topple to the right, and when it started to run out of steam, plopping into the cup.

Suddenly, I realized I wasn't visualizing anymore. I had hit the putt exactly as I had read it and it had gone into the cup for a birdie 3. Talk about getting a boost!

A Putting Tip

Before the gallery calms down and we go on to the next tee, let me discuss a point that I believe is significant in the putting game. I try very, very hard not to allow myself to develop any preferences as to the break of a putt. In other words, I refuse to allow myself to prefer a putt that breaks from right to left, or one that breaks from left to right.

The reason for this refusal is simple. I feel that you can develop too many mental blocks if you find that you prefer one or the other of the breaks. For instance, suppose you decide that you like to stroke those putts that break left to right. Then, when you get the right-to-left putt, you have a tendency to lack confidence in your stroke. Or even worse, if you get the putt that breaks as you prefer and you miss it, then you really get disturbed.

I won't allow any favorites on putts, and I think you would do well to adopt that attitude too. A putt is just a putt. The less I worry about which type I like best—"gimmies" excluded, of course—the better off I am.

NO. 13 (465 YARDS, PAR 4)

In the Rough Again

The wind was letting up more and more, and my adrenalin was gushing after the birdie at No. 12, so on my drive here I guess I let my hands get just a little bit ahead of the clubhead. I pushed the ball and it bounced into the edge of the right rough.

This was a new experience for me, because of the four fairways I had missed during the round, I had missed them all to the left. Yet, even from the right rough I faced a rather familiar problem. It was, as a matter of fact, similar to the shot I had on the hole before. I had a sailing lie, and there were lakes in front of the green. I was approximately 175 yards from the flag.

I selected a 7-iron, again allowing 20 or 25 yards for the anticipated sail out of the

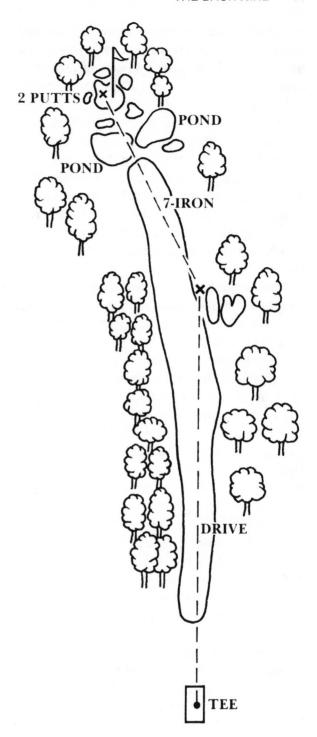

Hole No. 13   465 Yards, Par 4

This hole has a back tee from which the members play it as a par 5. From the par-4 tee, a good drive is to the right center of the fairway. This leaves a 175-yard approach iron shot to the green. Two ponds guard the front of the green, and the small putting surface is surrounded by traps.

Graham pushed his drive into the edge of the right rough and faced a second shot similar to the one he had hit on the previous hole. He hit a 7-iron that sailed and rolled 30 feet past the pin. He two-putted for a par 4.

rough. It was a fair lie, not good, but not bad. I played the ball up forward in my stance as before, and I hit with a sweeping motion in order to pick the ball out of the grass and get it in the air.

The shot had to be hit high if it was going to stay on the green. That's because this green had been very hard most of the week and what little wind there was came from directly behind me. I wasn't trying anything fancy on this shot. There was too much trouble on all sides. In addition to a couple of ponds in front, there are six bunkers around the green.

The important thing was to make sure I caught the ball solid coming out of the rough so I could get the distance required of the shot. My first thought was to hit the ball far enough to get over the water. Naturally, I would prefer being in the back trap rather than in the front water.

I hit the 7-iron shot and it carried the full 175 yards. The ball landed flag-high and rolled past the pin, maybe 30 feet, which was a good shot onto this green.

My Misread Putt

I hit the putt all right, but the moment I had it rolling, I realized I had misread the thing. When you are playing on greens that you do not play day in and day out, reading them sometimes can become incredibly difficult. A lot of times I've found it hard to tell whether a putt is up- or downhill. I know that sounds funny, but you might be surprised to discover how many times you think you are going one way, when you are really going another. When you are on strange, rolling greens, it is a good idea to walk off to the side of your putt, and bend down to see if the ball or the hole is higher.

Anyway, I misread the putt. I figured the ball to go to the right and it broke to the left.

I had a tap-in left, however, so I made my par 4.

NO. 14 (207 YARDS, PAR 3)

Designed For My Draw

This is an excellent par-3 hole, and from the tee you can see all sorts of trouble spots that you want to avoid. Luckily for me and my draw, the wind was light and from right to left. Also, the pin was placed on the left side of the green. This meant that with my normal draw I could play my shot to the center of the green and let the ball move right to left toward the cup.

This green has unusually deep rough around it and a half-dozen strategically located bunkers. I selected a 2-iron for my shot, knowing that with my routine swing and ball action I wouldn't have to bother with the trouble.

It was a good 2-iron shot. The ball reacted as anticipated, for it moved slightly toward the left and it wound up about 10 feet from the hole.

I studied this putt with particular care, after having misread the line on the preceding hole. On this putt I felt it would be a left-to-right break of between one and two inches. I hit the putt with perfect speed and it went squarely in the middle of the hole for a deuce.

This was my second birdie in three holes and I continued to be pumped up, for as I had walked off the 13th green, I had seen where Hubert had bogied two straight holes while I was going 3-4-2, birdie-par-birdie. So I had gained four shots on him, three shots in a two-hole stretch.

Now things were really beginning to look promising for me. I had played some tough holes under par and was stepping over putts with great confidence. This is the key to good putting—confidence.

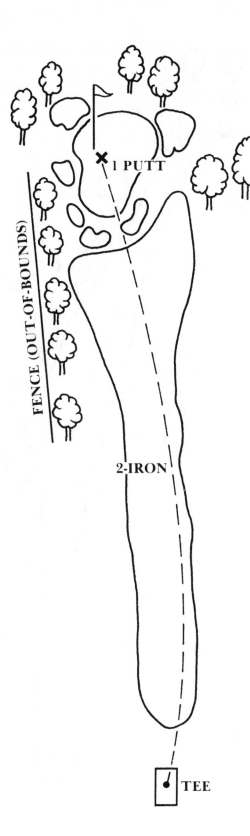

Hole No. 14   207 Yards, Par 3

This is an excellent par-3 hole, requiring a long iron or fairway wood to a well-bunkered green which slopes to the center. It was here that Tom Purtzer's tee shot went out of bounds in the heated fourth-round competition.

Graham's normal draw shot (right to left) was perfect for this day. He hit a 2-iron which curled toward the flag on the left side of the green. The ball stopped 10 feet from the cup, and he one-putted for a birdie 2.

NO. 15 (407 YARDS, PAR 4)

Three Out of Four

This hole offers a reasonable birdie opportunity if you can get the ball into the preferred spot off the tee. I hit one of my better drives of the week, unloading with a bit of draw on the ball.

The drive passed just to the right of center at the dogleg that breaks back to the left. It rolled on well past the fairway bunker at the left, and I wound up right in the middle of the fairway.

The flag was situated in a favorable position for me and my draw for the second straight hole. I was hitting into a bit of a breeze, and I figured the distance to the flag was something like 145 yards. I also could feel the excitement inside me, so I felt this emotional surge would offset whatever wind velocity there might be. I selected an 8-iron for the shot.

The green slopes quite sharply from back to front, and it had been rather soft in previous rounds. This meant that if I came up with the incorrect club selection, I could hit the green and conceivably spin back off the putting surface. In this situation, make sure you take enough club.

The 8-iron shot had the slightest bit of draw as it went toward the pin. The ball landed 15 feet to the right of the flag and really sat

Hole No. 15   407 Yards, Par 4

This is an unusually good par 4, with the premium drive passing just to the right of the bunker guarding the left corner of the dogleg. The green slopes severely from back to front. Shots can draw back several feet if hit with plenty of spin.

Graham's drive was a slight hook which continued well past the bunker and wound up in the center of the fairway. He has an 8-iron approach left. The ball hit and backed up, leaving him an 18-foot putt, breaking slightly to the left. He made the putt for a birdie 3.

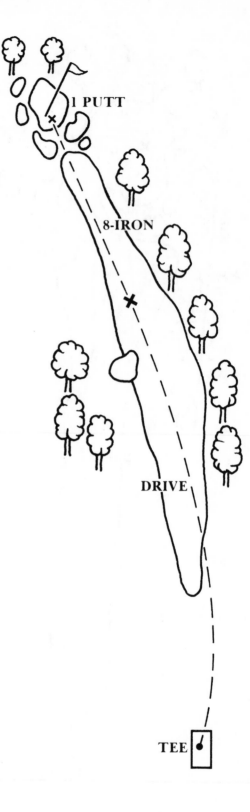

down well. As a matter of fact, it did what I figured it might do. It began backing up. It backed left and a little toward the hole. When it quit moving, I had about an 18-footer, slightly downhill.

This putt really required some reading, for when I first visualized the line, I got the ball to the cup and was maybe six inches below it. I took another look and this time I came up with a break of about a foot.

I hit the putt with the absolute best speed. It broke the full 12 inches and just barely got to the front rim of the cup as it fell in for another birdie.

That's three birdies in four holes and the next hole is a par 5. I can't wait to get to the tee!

NO. 16 (569 YARDS, PAR 5)

Trying to Settle Down

At this point, I had to start talking to myself, because that is one way to get settled down and not allow yourself to get in too big a hurry. This is a problem that occurs with many athletes. The urgency of a situation, the idea of "let's get on with it" or "let me hurry and hit the next shot" can spoil a round. This isn't just the U.S. Open players' problem, either. It can hurt you in a club event or in your weekend match. When you get things going well for you, don't ruin it by getting overanxious.

As I stood on the 16th tee, I kept saying to

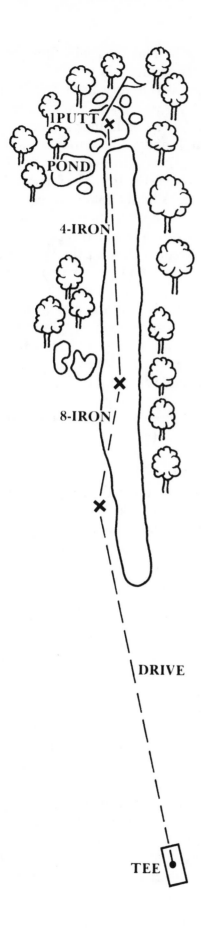

Hole No. 16   569 Yards, Par 5

The long hitters try to reach this green in two shots, but it requires a good drive to get to the flat landing area in the fairway. The second shot is blind and if off-line left, may find a pond or bunker just short of the green. The hole is quite straight away and the green is deceptive when putting to the left.

Graham pulled his drive into the left rough and because of a poor lie, played back to the fairway with an 8-iron. His third shot, hit with a 4-iron, stopped five feet past the pin. He made the putt for a birdie 4.

myself, "Think smart. Don't get too excited. Don't let your tempo get away from you."

If you don't use something like talking to yourself, everything speeds up and frequently you don't even realize it. You become so wrapped up in what's happening that you forget to think out each shot.

I had trouble driving on this par-5 hole all week, and in three rounds I had been in the fairway only once off the tee. Now the light wind was coming left to right and a little behind. I figured I needed a big drive in order to have a chance at reaching the green in two. On in two shots, of course, and I knew I had a great chance for another birdie.

I aimed the ball down the left edge of the fairway, planning to let the little breeze help the ball drift to the right. I hit the drive well, but if I had an unlucky bounce all day, it came on this drive.

The ball landed just about on the fairway-rough line and it kicked left, stopping about 10 feet into the rough. The ball wound up in a very difficult lie. It was down in the deep Bermuda grass, probably six inches deep. As much as I really wanted to hit the ball way down toward the green, I stuck to my rule of giving the trouble shot every consideration before deciding on a plan.

There was really no decision because of the lie, and now the most important part of the whole tournament was for me to get the ball out of that deep rough and back into the fairway. Hopefully, I could get it out far enough to reach the green on my third shot.

I went after the ball with an 8-iron and I hit the shot pretty well. The ball traveled maybe 110 yards, maybe less, but I did achieve my purpose. I got the ball back on the fairway where at least I had a chance to make it to the green on the third shot.

Rescued by My 4-Iron

My troubles seemed to be mounting now, for the pin was in an extremely tough location. It was tucked to the left and right behind a trap. My natural draw would help on the approach iron shot, but with the slightest miscalculation I could not only lose a chance at a birdie, but I might even wind up missing my par.

That would be disastrous, for I felt sure Hubert would come along in a few minutes and probably make a birdie. If I didn't birdie, or if I lost a shot to par, I would lose the advantages I had gained with my string of sub-par holes.

I estimated I was 195 to 200 yards from the flag and slightly downwind. That's just a little out of my normal 4-iron range, but because of the situation—the wind, downhill, and my adrenalin—I elected to try it with a 4-iron.

In my opinion, the 4-iron shot I hit was one of the best of my life. It certainly was the best of the tournament for me. I played the ball a little to the right of the flag, no more than five or six feet, actually. I kept thinking that in a situation like this—hitting a long iron shot under tremendous pressure—you should always hit the shot hard. If you try to hit it easy with the pressure on, more than likely you tend to quit a little. That's because you are all pumped up and your body wants to go after the shot hard, but your mind tells you to let off a little.

Invariably, you'll turn your hands over or hit "pushes" or "pulls." It is most important to remember that when the pressure is really on, try to select a club that gives you a chance to make a full shot. Don't try half shots or three-quarter shots. Try to hit these pressure shots hard. I think you will find you have much better results this way.

I hit the 4-iron very hard and it carried about 200 yards. This is a very long 4-iron shot for me. The ball landed about two feet from the hole and bounced maybe three more feet, leaving me a five-footer for a birdie.

On the 4-iron shot from the fairway I had a fairly flat lie, slightly uphill. When you hit a shot hard, you don't snap your wrists or pop your hands or make any special effort to hit the ball extremely hard at the bottom of the swing. You just build up the whole idea in your mind and in your swing. You start the club back slowly, as you should do on any shot, and then as you come back into the ball you work with a feeling of extra strength all over your body. But, beware of trying to make any single extra bit of "hit" at any specific point in the swing. If you try this, you are going to lose your balance, lose your timing, and not get a solid shot.

Pressure Builds

My putt was downhill with a little bit of break at the start. The ball began moving off to the left just slightly and then in the last six or seven inches it started to flatten out a little. It was a putt that you had to keep inside the right part of the hole. It was going to drift over to the center and straighten out the last few inches. That's what happened too, and with all the hollering that was going on, I knew it was adding to the pressure on Hubert.

He was over on the 13th green, not more than 30 yards from me. I saw that he was looking over a 4- or 5-footer for his par. The gallery at my green was making a lot of noise with its cheers, and I knew this was making his putt more difficult. He could now feel the pressure of someone coming up on him. He had had a good lead and could feel it slipping away. Things like 4- or 5-footers tend to magnify in your own mind under such circumstances, and later, of course, I was to learn that Hubert also had been told of a death threat on him.

I was feeling optimistic about my chances of winning now for I was playing ahead of the leader. Lots of times this is a real advantage. If you get a big charge going and are playing in front of the leader and you are coming up on him, you can heap pressure on him, especially if you can birdie some of those tough holes that he still has to play.

I try not to let knowledge of what others are doing affect my play if at all possible. The only time I think this knowledge should enter into your planning is when and if you decide you have to gamble. You should always play the golf course until you get down to the last few holes and need to gamble to try to win the tournament. In this situation, when you are making the big effort to win, you can't continue to play the same type of attack. You then must go after the leader. If you take a gamble and make it good, then the player coming along behind you must take the same gamble in an effort to stay ahead.

There is the other angle to this theory too, and that is that if you are keeping up with the other scores on the last few holes, you know that sometimes it is not necessary to gamble in order to win. This knowledge is vital in the latter stages of any event.

NO. 17 (354 YARDS, PAR 4)

A Memorable Hole

The 17th is an exceptionally narrow driving hole, and of course this means the tee shot is the key. During the week I had used a driver off the tee twice and had hit a 2-iron the other time. The one time I had used the iron, I had a 6-iron second shot. The other two times, when I had hit the driver, I had little sand iron shots to the green.

You must hold the ball to the left side of the fairway on the hole because the right side runs down into the rough. There are actually only about 15 yards of good landing area available, and the tee shot has to travel on the left side near a line of trees.

On the tee I debated whether I should hit the driver. I decided that if I hit it, I would be set up in good shape to make a birdie and have a super chance to win my second Open. On the other hand, a 2-iron shot off the tee would have to be hit extremely well to put me in good position in the fairway, where I still would have—at best—a 7-iron shot to the green. That certainly would not assure me of a good birdie opportunity.

I elected to use the driver, and when I made contact with the ball I felt as though I quit on the shot. My hands came over real fast and the ball was pulled, much the same as I had done on the first two holes when I had knocked drives into the left trees.

Here, the ball clipped the limbs coming out of the chute and it kicked back to the left into the trees, leaving me a very difficult, long shot. Nevertheless, I could have been in even worse shape. I felt I was fortunate to have any kind of shot out of the trees.

The Shot Seen 'Round the World

When I got to the ball, I saw that it was in bare ground with a low-hanging tree limb about 25 yards in front of me. The bare-ground lie was the only type of lie I could have to possibly get the ball out and onto the green. Had I been in the rough, in the grass I mean, I would have had to chip the ball out into the fairway, because in tall grass the ball would have jumped up in the air the moment I hit it. Then, of course, it would have been in the limbs of the tree. By having a bare-ground lie, I knew I could hit the ball low and not worry about getting it out of the forest and advancing it along the fairway.

I did have to put a pretty good hook on the ball to get it around the tree ahead of me. Standing back in the trees, I looked straight out of the opening and saw the sand traps to the right side of the green and a creek also on the right. If I allowed the hook to come too soon and hit the tree, I might come back in the woods or glance off and go across the fairway, down the slope, and into the water. This was the immediate goal, to get the ball

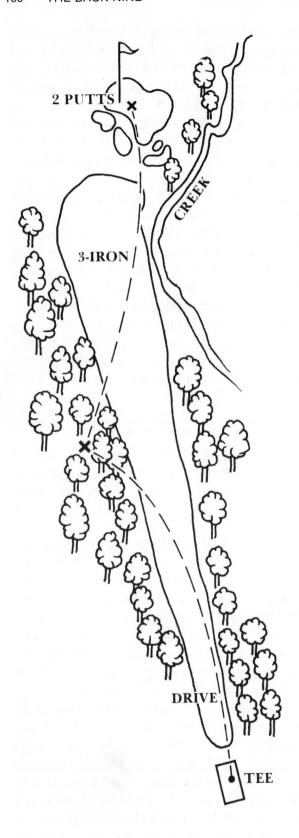

2 PUTTS

CREEK

3-IRON

DRIVE

TEE

Hole No. 17   354 Yards, Par 4

The tee shot is the key here, on what many describe as one of the better short holes in golf. Players frequently use a long iron or fairway wood off this tee. Tree trouble is left and right at the start. The green is well trapped and a definite slope to the right leads down the bank to a creek. The green is small, and with the pin on the left side of the green it is difficult to get an approach iron shot close to the hole.

Graham hoped to hold his drive against a left-to-right wind. The ball clipped the trees on the left and kicked into the woods. His rolling-hook 3-iron shot was the most spectacular of the tournament. It stopped eight feet from the pin. Graham two-putted for a par 4.

out of the trees, but not let it go right because of the traps and creek.

I continued to utilize my trouble-shot strategy and put into focus everything that I thought could happen. I determined I didn't want to put the ball into the right bunkers. The pin was on the far left, and a shot from any of the right bunkers would be about a 125-foot blast. That's one of the toughest shots in golf, so I wanted to avoid it if at all possible. I surely didn't want to go right of the traps or I would be in the creek.

Finally, I decided to make sure that if I missed the green, I would miss it to the left. In other words, if I overhooked the shot from out of the trees, about the worst thing I could do would be to hit the ball into the left trap. There, the blast would be 40 feet or less, and that's a decent shot from the sand.

Hopefully I could hit the ball out with a rolling hook and bring it in to land just on the front edge of the green between the traps. The green rolled toward the left, and that's where the pin was situated.

I selected a 3-iron and figured I had 170 yards to the front edge of the green. When I want to play a big, rolling hook, I like to open my stance a little and turn my left foot well out toward the target and draw it off the line of play.

This stance allows me to move my left side out of the way and let my hands pronate over on top of the ball. This keeps the ball low and allows it to hook. I play the ball forward on the shot. If I play it too far back for this stance, I may get out of the way so fast with my left side that I get a push shot without any hook.

I hit the shot good and solid and I knew it was going to carry at least 170 yards. I really felt I might have hit it too hard. The ball started out low and hooking and then the crowd rushed in front of me to watch. I never really saw the shot until I watched some television replays of it.

As it turned out, the ball stayed under the trees perfectly, had the proper hook on it and just the right distance. It landed short of the green, kicked to the left and started rolling along the contour of the putting surface right toward the flag. It stopped pin high to the right of the flag, some eight feet from the cup.

How Could I Have Missed the Putt?

I looked at the putt from all sides and figured the ball would break just a little to the left. Some of my friends have said they thought I hit the putt too quickly. Others say I took too much time with it. There are those who claim I pulled the putt, while others swear from their vantage I pushed it. Whatever, I missed it.

I really felt that I hit the putt within the normal length of time for me. I try to putt and hit all shots on a rhythm of 1-2-3. I address the ball. I look down, or I look down the fairway. I look at the flag, or I look at the cup three times. Then, I try to play the shot. If I am not ready to hit, I back off and try to start this 1-2-3 rhythm over again.

I felt as though I stayed on the rhythm well, for I am a big believer that in pressure situations this routine is important. I tried to play the putt to the right center of the cup. I misread it a little bit, but I also pulled the putt. That's what really hurt, because the putt broke more to the left than I thought it would.

Still, when I first looked up, the putt was about 2 feet short of the hole. It was still rolling inside the left side of the hole, whereas I had read it to be in the dead center of the cup. When it started to break, I knew I had missed it.

Walking off the green I told my caddy, "I cannot believe I missed that putt." Then I turned around and looked back down at those trees and commented, "But, how could I possibly complain about a par?"

It was the best trouble shot I had ever hit in competition. Seldom does a day pass that somebody on tour fails to mention it. When I returned to Nashville a couple of days after the Open, a friend of mine met me and said he had come within an inch or two of filing suit against me.

"How's that?" I asked him.

"Well, when you hit that ball out of those trees on 17, and it wound up eight feet from the hole, I jumped out of my television chair and landed on my dog's leg. He ran off howling and limping. If my dog had died, I surely would have sued you."

Another Nashville buddy said he really felt he had cost me the Open this time.

"How do you figure that?" I asked.

"When you were back there in the forest on No. 17, I was sitting here at home watching on television. I said a little prayer that you would make a par from there. If I had known how good a shot you were going to hit, I could just as easily have prayed for a birdie."

People have asked me if I wake up screaming at night about missing the putt. Not really, because I believe things even up, and while I missed maybe a very makeable putt on the 17th, I hit one of the most satisfying putts in my life on the very next hole. They are the kinds of putts I dream about. The good ones.

NO. 18 (449 YARDS, PAR 4)

A Nearly Perfect Drive

After having hit some very poor drives during the day, I got everything together on this one and drove the ball almost perfectly. Had it been 10 feet to the left, I would call it the ultimate drive for me.

This hole doglegs to the right and is an extremely difficult finishing hole. Throughout the tournament many players complained of its degree of difficulty. The approach shots often were hit with fairway woods or long irons, and they were hit to an elevated green with the severest slope on the course.

I hit a cut shot with the driver. The wind had let up almost completely by now. The ball "blew out of the chute," dropped down a little hill on the right, and rolled onto a plateau-type landing area that is about 10 yards long and 30 yards wide. The position left me with a shot of about 150 yards up a very severe hill.

"Double-Cross"

In determining my club for the approach shot, I added 15 or 20 yards for the hill and

Hole No. 18   449 Yards, Par 4

This dogleg right is a superb finishing hole, demanding pin point driving accuracy and an approach shot to an elevated green. The green is the fastest and most severely sloping one on the course. When the cup is located toward the front of the green the break is particularly severe.

Graham's drive was moving left to right slightly. It kicked almost to the bottom of the hill, stopping on a small plateau not more than 10 yards long and 30 yards wide. Graham's approach shot was 150 yards, but up a severe hill. The pin was to the right, and trees at the dogleg prevented Graham from hitting straight toward the flag. His attempt to cut the ball failed and he was left with a 70-foot putt with a break of at least 15 feet. He two-putted for his par 4.

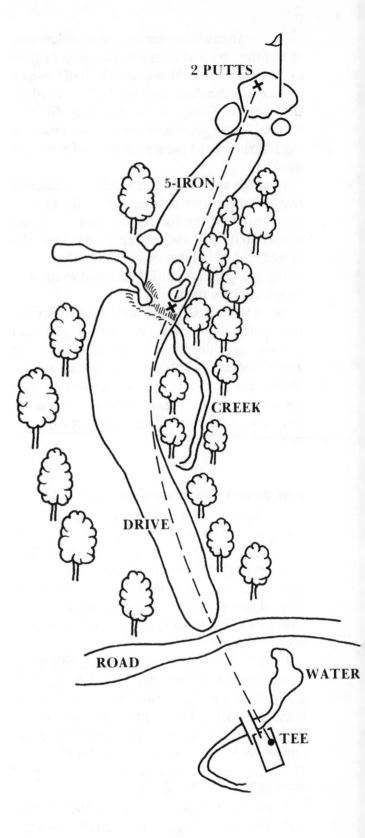

about five yards for the easy breeze. I selected a 5-iron for the shot. My plan was to hit a nice smooth shot with just a little cut on it to hold against the light wind.

The pin placement was on the extreme righthand side of the green, and trees at the right side of the fairway prevented me from going directly toward the flag. I had hit this little cut shot two or three times with considerable success during the round so I had a lot of confidence that I could hit it one more time.

Instead, I hit what I call a "double-cross." I was aiming a little left of the center of the green and I hit the ball to the left of that. It meant I wound up with a 70-foot putt.

In analyzing my 5-iron shot, I felt that as I got to the ball my left side and my legs slowed down and my hands caught up quickly. When I was hitting into the shot, instead of my legs driving forward to get my weight up and over to the left side, my legs were too slow-moving. The weight stayed on the right side, really on my right foot. This meant that my hands turned over on top of the ball and pulled the shot. Instead of putting the desired cut on the ball, I yanked it left.

The Grand Finale

When I got to the ball on the far left side of the green, I looked at the big scoreboard there and saw Hubert was on No. 15. I felt if he birdied the 16th (the par 5) I was out of it. I figured he faced a very possible bogey here on the 18th—just as I did. I realized that whatever chances I had were hanging on whether I could two-putt from 70 feet across this severely breaking green.

I really didn't think about making the putt, because that falls into the miracle category.

From my position, I saw the pin way over on the other side of the green sitting on a little ledge. Between my ball and the pin were a couple of knobs, a dip or two, and a slope creating a break of perhaps 15 feet from left to right.

I had a very unusual sensation when I hit the putt. The crowd of fans, many of whom had watched putts on this green for hours, let out a big groan the moment I hit the ball.

I thought, "Oh, my gosh. I have played much too much break because the spectators know this putt. They've seen it plenty of times today and they know how it breaks."

Well, it rolled along for about 40 feet and when it got to the top of the last ridge, it began dropping to the right just as I had figured it would. It turned down the hill and went down into a gully and began picking up speed again. It was breaking tremendously now. The groans turned into cheers, because the ball had begun to trickle directly toward the cup. It stopped 12 inches from the hole.

I believe it is the best lag putt I have ever hit. I had visualized the break perfectly and had the speed of the green figured too. It was a fantastic feeling to walk across the green and know that I had a par locked up. Now I was the leader in the clubhouse, with a chance to win my second U.S. Open.

It was a most exciting back nine for me. I shot 31 and came from seven shots off the lead with seven holes to go. It made for a beautiful day and a wonderful tournament. Best of all, that last big putt was one of those shots that so many golfers hit on the last hole of the day, the one that brings them back tomorrow.

I couldn't wait until the next tournament began, so I could play again.

Index